British Flags & Emblems

Graham Bartram

About the Author

Graham Bartram is the General Secretary of the Flag Institute, Secretary-General for Congresses of FIAV (*Fédération internationale des associations vexillologiques* - the international flag organization) and a consultant to HM Government on flags. He was born in Montrose, Scotland, but grew up in Perth, Dundee, Belfast, Accra, Lagos, Reigate, Montrose and Chesterfield. He has been interested in flags since living amongst the many embassies and high commissions of Accra, the capital of Ghana. His professional interest in flags started when he took on the task of providing the flags for a new electronic atlas of the World, *3D Atlas*. By the end of the project he had managed to include 700 flags! He has since worked on several new national flags, including advising the UN on Bosnia & Herzegovina and designing the flags of Antarctica and Tristan da Cunha. He now edits *BR20 Flags of all Nations* for the Ministry of Defence.

The author would like to thank the following for their help and encouragement in the creation of this book:

HRH The Duke of Edinburgh for his comments and corrections, Robin Ashburner, Malcolm Farrow, Michael Faul, Bruce Nicholls, David Protheroe, Chris Rickard, Ian Sumner, Nick Weekes, Hugh Witherow and many other members of the Flag Institute, Jonathan Spencer (Deputy Comptroller) of the Lord Chamberlain's Office, Henry Bedingfeld (York Herald) of the College of Arms, Robin Blair (Lord Lyon) and Elizabeth Roads (Lyon Clerk) of the Lyon Office, Commodore Tony Johnstone-Burt, past Captain of HMS *Montrose*, Jenny Wraight of the Admiralty Library, Christopher Allan of Ede & Ravenscroft, Richard Yeoward of the Royal Dee Yacht Club, His Grace The Duke of Norfolk, His Grace The Duke of Montrose, The Macneil of Barra and Macdonald of Castle Camus for their kind permission to include their personal armorial flags, and the many organizations and associations which provided information on their flags and emblems.

Contents

FLAG INSTITUTE
www.flaginstitute.org

The Old Colours of the Forty-third

A moth-eaten rag on a worm-eaten pole,
It does not look likely to stir a man's soul,
'Tis the deeds that were done 'neath the moth-eaten rag
When the pole was a staff, and the rag was a flag

General Sir Edward Hamley (1824-1893)

Foreword by HRH The Duke of Edinburgh KG KT

"For as much as men in all ages have made for themselves signs and emblems of their allegiance to their rulers, and of their duty to uphold those laws and institutions which God's providence has called them to obey; we, following this ancient and honoured custom, stand before God this day to ask his blessing on these Colours, and pray that they may be an abiding symbol of our duty towards our Sovereign and our Country, and a sign of our resolve to guard, preserve, and sustain the great traditions of bravery and self-sacrifice of which we are the proud inheritors."

So begins the service of consecration of Colours about to be presented to Regiments and other Service units. Regimental Colours are very special flags and their original purpose was to identify the position of the Regiment in the thick of battle. Indeed, all the flags shown in this book serve the same purpose of identification, whether it be nations, individuals or organisations. For that reason alone, it is most important to ensure that these identifying symbols are correctly displayed on appropriate occasions.

Graham Bartram, the author of this most valuable book, has taken infinite pains to collect and explain a very large number of British flags and emblems presently in use. Symbols mean a lot to people and they can be deeply offended if they are depicted or used in the wrong way. I hope that this book will serve to answer many questions about the origin, design and display of British Flags and Emblems.

Philip

British Flags and Emblems
by Graham Bartram

This book is dedicated to my parents, Clive and Sandra Bartram, for giving me the confidence to follow my own path, to John Newmark, a great teacher who started me on this journey, and to William Crampton who opened up the world of flags to me.

First published in the United Kingdom by The Flag Institute and Tuckwell Press in 2004

ISBN 1-86232-297-X

Printed and bound in the European Union by Gráficas Santamaría S.A.

Introduction

The national flag of the United Kingdom is the Union Flag or Union Jack. The original design dates back to 1606 in the reign of James VI of Scotland and I of England and was used until 1801 when the current design was introduced. So in 2001 the modern Union Flag celebrated its 200th anniversary and in 2006 the original Union Flag celebrates its 400th anniversary.

This guide to the many flags and emblems of the United Kingdom has been produced to mark these events. It covers the national flag, the Royal Standards, the national flags of the Constituent Countries, the Crown Dependencies and the Overseas Territories, the origins of these flags and the protocol governing their use (ie. when and how they should be flown). It is intended for use by Government and Executive departments, British overseas missions, Local Government, schools, corporations, businesses and private individuals.

The guide has been produced by the Flag Institute, the United Kingdom's flag organization, in consultation with the Lord Chamberlain's department, the College of Arms, and the Office of the Lord Lyon.

The National Flag of the United Kingdom of Great Britain and Northern Ireland

A Short History of the Union Flag

In March 1603 Elizabeth I of England died without an heir, and her Ministers invited James VI of Scotland to accept the Crown of England. The two countries remained independent under a single Monarch, James VI and I, who called his new combined realm the Kingdom of Great Britain (after the name of the mainland of the British Isles).

The 1606 Pattern Union Flag

In 1606, following some altercations over flags between English and Scottish ships, James VI and I issued the following proclamation:

> A Proclamation declaring what Flags South and North Britains shall bear at Sea
>
> Whereas some difference has arisen between our Subjects of South and North Britain, Travelling by Sea, about the bearing of their flags, for avoiding of all such contentions hereafter, We have with the advice of our Council ordered That from henceforth all our subjects of the Isle and Kingdom of Great Britain and the Members thereof shall bear in their maintop the Red Cross, commonly called St George's Cross, and the White Cross, commonly called St Andrew's Cross, joined together, according to a form made by our Heralds and sent by Us to our Admiral to be published to our said Subjects. And in their foretop Our Subjects of South Britain shall wear the Red Cross only as they were wont, and our Subjects of North Britain in their Foretop the White Cross only as they were accustomed. Wherefore We will and command all our Subjects to be conformable and obedient to this Our Order, and that from henceforth they do not use to bear their flags in any other Sort, as they will answer the contrary at their Peril.
>
> Given at our Palace of Westminster the 12th. day of April in the 4th. year of our Reign of Great Britain France and Ireland Anno Domini 1606.

The exact design that accompanied the proclamation has been lost. Several designs are known to have been considered, including quartering the flags of England and Scotland (as the Royal Standard is quartered), and putting the two side-by-side, but the chosen design was a fimbriated (edged in a contrasting colour) St. George's Cross over the St. Andrew's Cross, as shown here.

Some Scots vessels used an unofficial version where the St. Andrew's Cross was superimposed on the St. George's Cross. The width of the white line (or fimbriation) around the St. George's Cross has also been a matter of debate. Actual flags from the period suggest that the fimbriation was quite wide. The shade of blue started as a sky blue, but gradually became darker over the centuries.

In 1634, after some disputes concerning saluting ships in the Channel, Charles I partially repealed his father's proclamation:

> A Proclamation appointing the Flags, as well for our Navy Royal as for the Ships of our Subjects of South and North Britain
>
> We taking into Our Royal consideration that it is meet for the Honour of Our own Ships in Our Navy Royal and of such other Ships as are or shall be employed in Our immediate Service, that the same be by their Flags distinguished from the ships of any other of Our Subjects, do hereby strictly prohibit and forbid that none of Our Subjects, of any of Our Nations and Kingdoms, shall from henceforth presume to carry the Union Flag in the Main top, or other part of any of their Ships (that is) S. Georges Cross and S. Andrews Cross joined together upon pain of Our high displeasure, but that the same Union Flag be still reserved as an ornament proper for Our own Ships and Ships in Our immediate Service and Pay, and none other.
>
> And likewise Our further will and pleasure is, that all the other Ships of Our Subjects of England or South Britain bearing flags shall from henceforth carry the Red-Cross, commonly called S. George his Cross, as of old time hath been used; And also that all other ships of Our Subjects of Scotland or North Britain shall henceforth carry the White Cross commonly called S. Andrews Cross, Whereby the several Shipping may thereby be distinguished and We thereby

Unofficial 1606 Scottish Union Flag

the better discern the number and goodness of the same. Wherefore We will and straitly command all Our Subjects forthwith to be conformable and obedient to this Our Order, as they will answer the contrary at their perils.

Given at Our Court at Greenwich this fifth day of May in the tenth year of our Reign of England Scotland France and Ireland, Defender of the Faith &c.

To this day civilian vessels are not permitted to use the Union Jack. They have their own Jack (a white bordered Union Jack - see page 74) and the courtesy flag for foreign vessels is an appropriately coloured ensign (red for civil vessels and white for naval vessels).

The execution of Charles I on 30th January 1649 brought an end to the union of the Crowns of England and Scotland. The Union Flag no longer made sense so the English Parliament ordered the Admiralty to choose a new design. This was to be the first of several designs used until the restoration of Charles II in May 1660 restored the Union and the pre-1649 flags.

In 1707, Queen Anne completed the task that James had started - the complete union of England and Scotland. The first article of the Treaty of Union stated that the flag would be the crosses of St. George and St. Andrew conjoined in such a manner as the Queen saw fit. Queen Anne decided to keep the existing design.

Until 1801 Ireland was a separate kingdom. In 1800 an Act of Union was passed to create the new United Kingdom of Great Britain and Ireland, to come into effect on 1st January 1801. The College of Arms designed a new flag with the Cross of St. Patrick counter-changed with the Cross of St. Andrew. The inclusion of St. Patrick's Cross is of interest as St. Patrick was not martyred and therefore

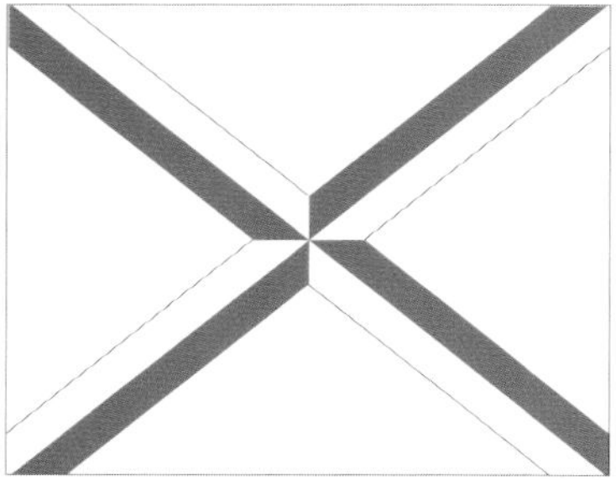

The Crosses of St. Andrew and St. Patrick Counter-changed

did not have a cross. The red saltire on white was the emblem of the powerful Irish Fitzgerald family and was chosen by the heralds of the College of Arms as a convenient symbol for Ireland.

The independence in 1922 of the southern part of Ireland as the Irish Free State (later the Republic of Ireland) did not result in any change to the Union Flag.

The Original 1801 Pattern of the Union Flag

The Proportions of the Union Flag

Over the years the flag changed shape to its current proportions. This was caused by default by the decrease in the width of the cloth (the breadth) used to make the flags, rather than a deliberate decision to alter the proportions. In 1687, Samuel Pepys, then Secretary of the Admiralty, had specified the size of flags as half a yard (eighteen inches) long for each breadth (then eleven inches) wide, giving proportions of 11:18. During the eighteenth century the width of the material became narrower (ten inches) but the length stayed the same, so the proportions changed to 10:18 or 5:9. Around 1837, the fabric width was reduced again, this time to nine inches, resulting in proportions of 9:18 or 1:2. This is the specification that is still used today. Modern British naval flags are still specified by breadths.

The Modern Union Flag

For the other national flags, the College of Arms recommends 3:5 as a sensible shape. This gives a flag that is close to the 'Golden Rectangle', an aethestically pleasing shape. The Office of the Lord Lyon gives 4:5 as the 'best' shape for Scotland's flag, the St. Andrew's Cross. Armorial banners work best in a square or 4:5 shape. These are also the shapes of military Colours.

The Union Jack or Union Flag?

The Union Jack and Jack Staff in the bows of HMS *Montrose*

When the 'Union Jack' was first introduced, in 1606, it was known simply as 'the British flag' or 'the flag of Britain'.

The first use of the name 'Union' appears in 1625. There are various theories which explain how it became known as the 'Union Jack', but most of the evidence points to the name being derived from the use of the word 'jack' as a diminutive. This word was in use before 1600 to describe a small flag flown from the small mast on the bowsprit, and by 1627 it appears that a small version of the Union Flag was commonly flown in this position. For some years it was called just 'the Jack', or 'Jack flag', or 'the King's Jack', but by 1674, while formally referred to as 'His Majesty's Jack', it was commonly called the Union Jack, and this was officially acknowledged.

In the 18th century the small mast on the bowsprit was replaced by staysails on the stays between the bowsprit and the foremast. By this time the Ensign had become the principal naval distinguishing flag, so it became the practice to fly the Union Jack only in harbour, on a specially rigged staff in the bows of the ships, the jack staff. It should be noted that the jack flag had existed for over a hundred and fifty years before the jack staff came into being, and thus its name was related to its size rather than to the position in which it was flown.

It is often stated that the Union Flag should only be described as the Union Jack when flown in the bows of a warship, but this is a relatively recent idea. From early in its life the Admiralty itself frequently referred to the flag as the Union Jack, whatever its use. This was given Parliamentary approval on 14th July 1908 when it was stated in a parliamentary answer by the Earl of Crewe, speaking on behalf of HM Government, that "the Union *Jack* should be regarded as the national flag".

Specifications of the National Flags

The Union Flag is normally twice as long as it is wide, a ratio of 1:2. In the United Kingdom land flags are normally 3:5 (ie. 5 units long for every 3 units wide). The Union Flag can also be made in this shape, but is 1:2 for most purposes. Flags that have the Union Flag in the canton should always be 1:2, to preserve the square fly area where the badge is sited.

The three component crosses that make up the Union Flag are sized as follows: the St. George's Cross is $\frac{1}{5}$ of the flag's width (the shorter side) wide with a $\frac{1}{15}$ flag width white fimbriation; the St. Andrew's Cross is $\frac{1}{5}$ flag width wide overall, the broader white diagonal is $\frac{1}{10}$ flag width, the red diagonal is $\frac{1}{15}$ flag width and the narrow white diagonal is $\frac{1}{30}$ flag width. The centre-lines of the diagonals should meet in the centre of the flag, as shown by the dotted line in the diagram.

The three flags of the constituent nations are shown at 3:5 as they are normally used as land flags, but if made at 1:2 the crosses retain their thickness, but the dragon on the Welsh flag should be placed centrally, not stretched. When the red or blue ensigns are defaced by a badge it is normally placed centrally in the square of the fly, the centring being visual or aesthetic rather than mathematical.

Note for Diagrams:

The Pantone colour references should be compared with an actual Pantone colour chart for production purposes. Allowance should be made for the type of material being used (fabric density, etc.). The final printed item should closely match the sample given in the Pantone chart.

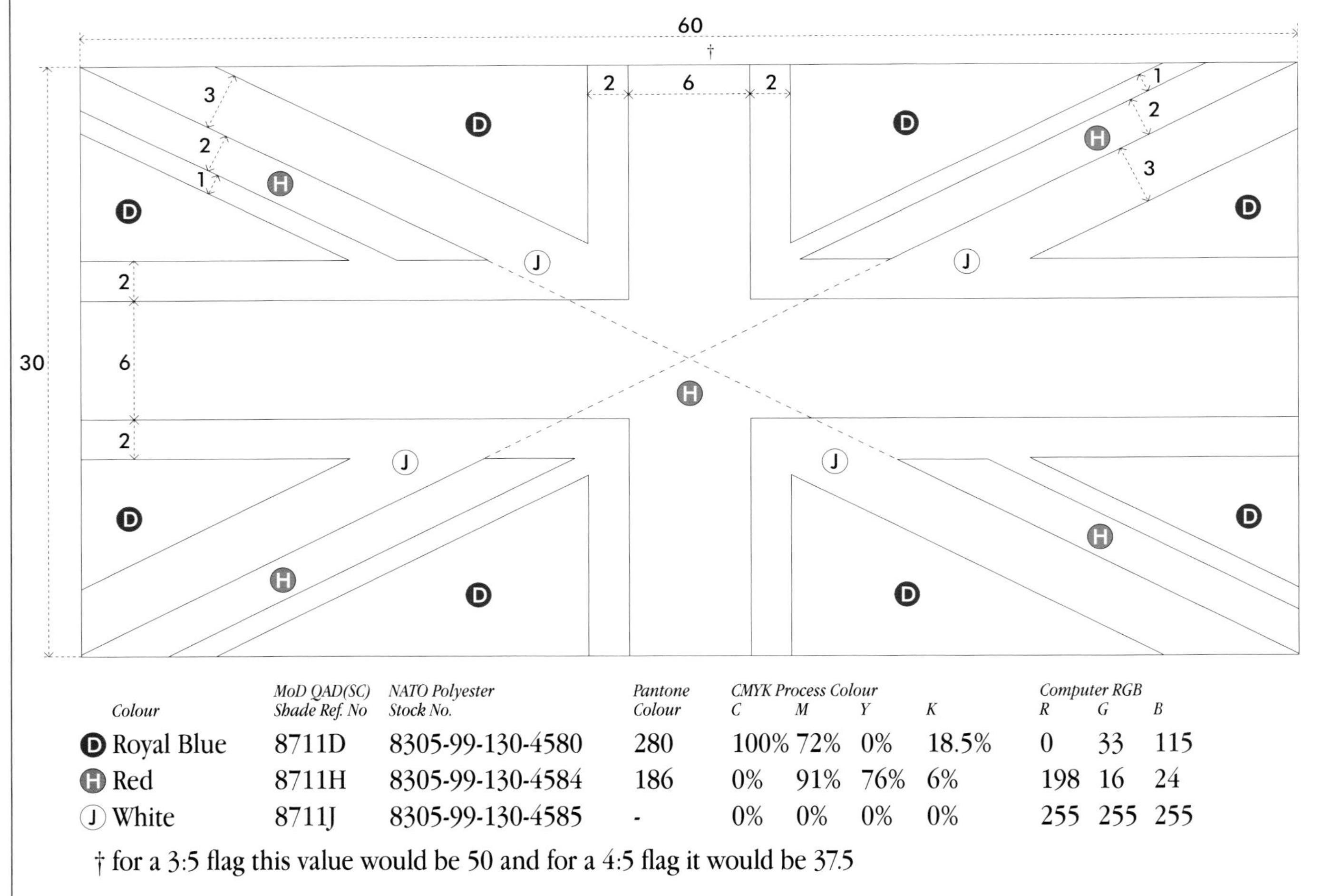

Colour	MoD QAD(SC) Shade Ref. No	NATO Polyester Stock No.	Pantone Colour	CMYK Process Colour C	M	Y	K	Computer RGB R	G	B
D Royal Blue	8711D	8305-99-130-4580	280	100%	72%	0%	18.5%	0	33	115
H Red	8711H	8305-99-130-4584	186	0%	91%	76%	6%	198	16	24
J White	8711J	8305-99-130-4585	-	0%	0%	0%	0%	255	255	255

† for a 3:5 flag this value would be 50 and for a 4:5 flag it would be 37.5

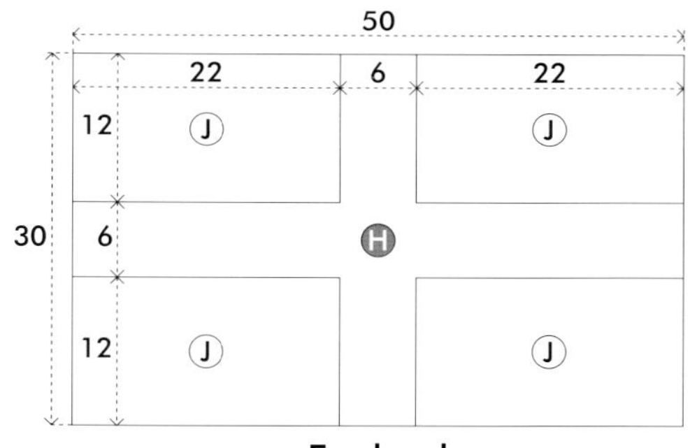

England

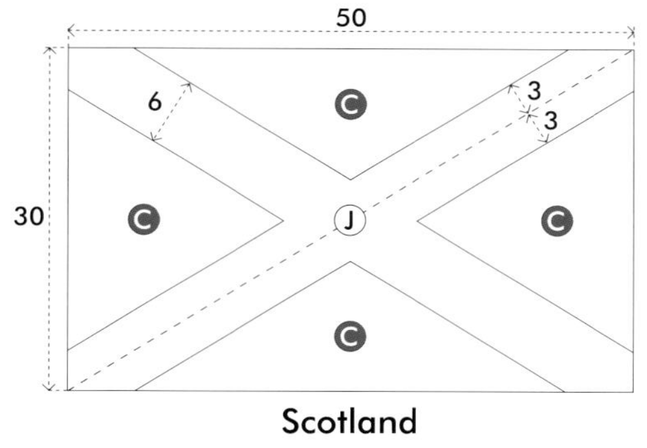

Scotland

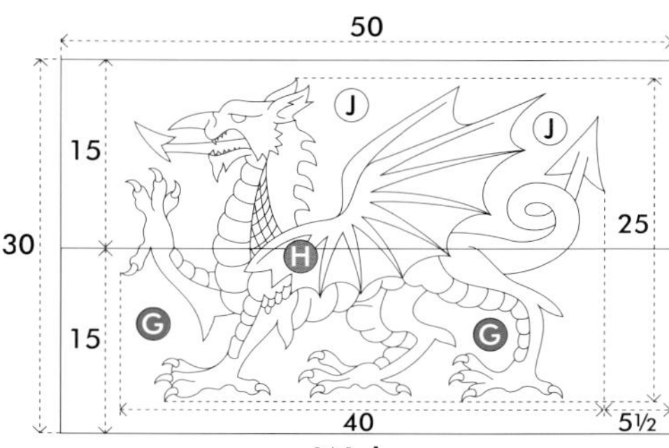

Wales

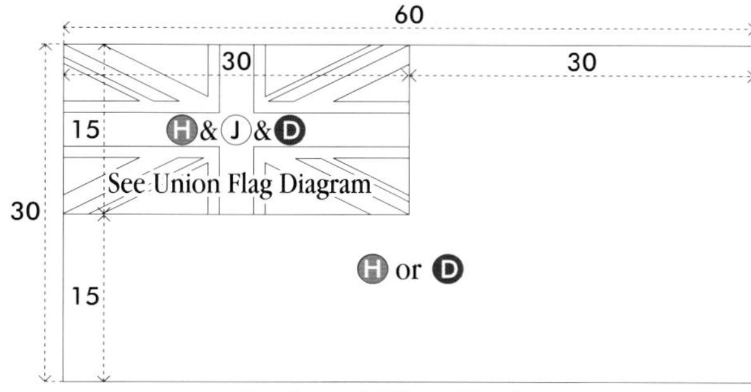

Red and Blue Ensigns

Colour	MoD QAD(SC) Shade Ref. No	NATO Polyester Stock No.	Pantone Colour	CMYK Process Colour C	M	Y	K	Computer RGB R	G	B
C Saltire Blue	8711C	8305-99-130-4579	300	100%	43%	0%	0%	0	93	159
G Green	8711G	8305-99-130-4583	354	91%	0%	83%	0%	0	139	77

England - St. George's Cross

Scotland - St. Andrew's Cross

Wales - The Red Dragon

Flags of Constituent Nations, Crown Dependencies and Overseas Territories

Three of the four constituent countries of the United Kingdom, the Crown Dependencies and the UK's Overseas Territories have their own national flags. These take precedence immediately after the Union Flag. The flags of England and Scotland are amongst the oldest in the world that are still in use.

England's flag dates back to the crusades. St. George was a very popular saint with the early crusaders, and they brought his cult back with them. The flag is based on the red crosses worn by the crusaders on their surcoats. The earliest record of its use in its current form is in 1277, in the reign of Edward I.

Scotland's flag is the Cross (or more accurately "saltire") of St. Andrew. In legend it dates back to the Battle of Athelstaneford in the 9th century when the Pictish king Angus MacFergus credited St. Andrew with his victory over the Saxon Athelstan. The clouds formed a white cross in the sky to signal St. Andrew's support of the Picts and the Saxons lost heart. Since the 11th century the white or silver saltire has been the symbol of the Scots. The blue background dates back to at least the 15th century.

Wales' flag is *Y Draig Goch* "The Red Dragon". The red dragon symbol dates back to the 4th century and in the 7th century Cadwaladr, Prince of Gwynedd, adopted it as his emblem. Green and white were the colours of the Welsh Prince Llewellyn. The Tudors used the same colours and adopted the red dragon as one of the supporters of the Royal Arms. The current design was introduced in 1959.

Northern Ireland is currently without a national flag, pending a new design to mark the resumption of self-rule.

The three Crown Dependencies of the Isle of Man, Jersey and Guernsey all have their own flags. Alderney, part of the Bailiwick of Guernsey, also has its own flag. Jersey and Guernsey have government Blue Ensigns which are flown by the islands' fishery protection and harbour vessels, and the Isle of Man and Guernsey have their own civil ensigns for use by vessels registered on the islands. Those registered in Jersey use an undefaced Red Ensign.

Jersey - Government Ensign

Jersey

Guernsey

Guernsey - Civil Ensign
(the Blue Ensign has the same design)

Alderney

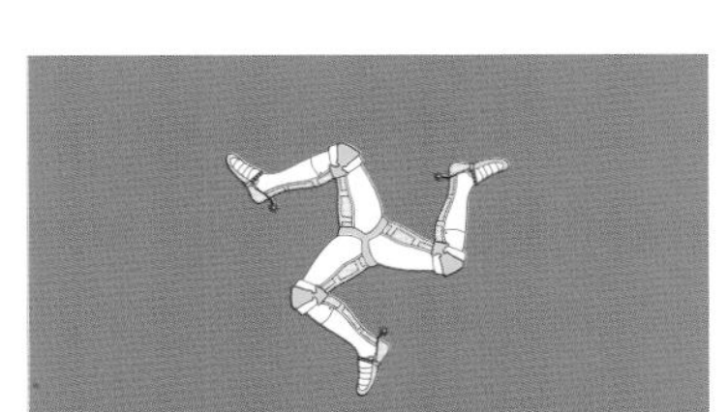

Isle of Man

Isle of Man - Civil Ensign

The United Kingdom's Overseas Territories each have flags of their own. Most of these are blue with the Union Flag in the canton and the coat-of-arms in the fly. Bermuda's flag has a red background instead of blue; the British Indian Ocean Territory has a wavy blue and white striped background, and the British Antarctic Territory has a white background. Gibraltar uses a banner of its arms as its flag, but also has a Blue Ensign for use at sea.

Bermuda, the Cayman Islands, the Falkland Islands and Gibraltar all have their own shipping registers and, apart from Bermuda that already used a Red Ensign, have been granted their own defaced Red Ensigns under the Merchant Shipping Act 1995. These match the Blue Ensigns, except Gibraltar's which is defaced by the modern arms of Gibraltar.

The Cayman Islands and Falkland Islands also use the original flag design with smaller arms on a white disc.

Anguilla

British Indian Ocean Territory

Bermuda

British Virgin Islands

British Antarctic Territory

Cayman Islands

Falkland Islands

Montserrat

South Georgia & South Sandwich Islands

Gibraltar

Pitcairn Islands

Tristan da Cunha (a dependency of Saint Helena)

Gibraltar - Civil Ensign

Saint Helena & Dependencies

Turks & Caicos Islands

The flag badges of the Overseas Territories are shown here enlarged to show the detail.

The newer badges, such as British Antarctic Territory and Tristan da Cunha, tend to show the whole armorial achievement, while the older badges show only the shield, or the shield with a motto. BIOT has the only non-armorial badge.

The flag of the Governor, Commissioner or Administrator of each territory shows these same badges surrounded by a garland, in the centre of a Union Flag (see page 58).

When the flags of the British Virgin Islands and Montserrat are used vertically, eg. indoors, the arms should be rotated so that they remain upright. The other badges can either remain as they would normally be or rotate in a similar manner.

Anguilla

British Antarctic Territory

British Virgin Islands

Bermuda

British Indian Ocean Territory

Cayman Islands

Falkland Islands

Montserrat

Saint Helena

Tristan da Cunha

Gibraltar

Pitcairn Islands

South Georgia & South Sandwich Islands

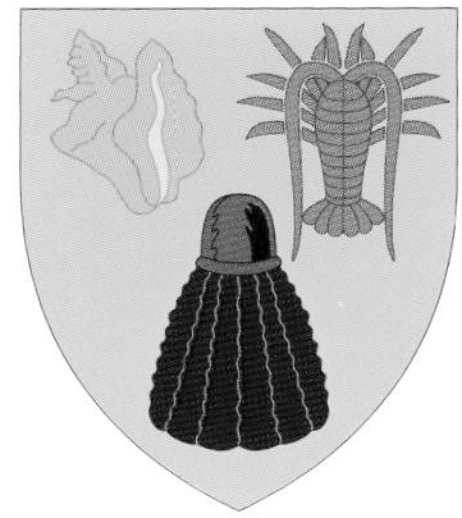
Turks & Caicos Islands

The Flag Etiquette of the United Kingdom

The National Flags of the United Kingdom (ie. the Union Flag and the flags of England, Scotland and Wales) should be displayed only in a manner befitting the national emblems; they should not be subjected to indignity and should not normally be displayed in a position inferior to any other flag or ensign. The National Flags should always be flown aloft and free.

It is improper to use any of the National Flags as a table or seat cover or as a masking for boxes, barriers, or intervening space between floor and ground level on a dais or platform. The use of any of the National Flags to cover a statue, monument or plaque for an unveiling ceremony is not common practice and is discouraged.

The National Flags should never be flown in a dilapidated or damaged condition, or when soiled. To do so is to show disrespect for the nations they represent.

Displaying the Flag

This flag is upside down!

Flags are normally flown from sunrise to sunset. Flags may be flown by night as well as by day as long as they are properly illuminated at all times, preferably by spotlight.

No permission is necessary to fly the National Flags and they are explicitly excluded from planning and advertising regulations (although flagpoles are not).

Important: the Union Flag has a correct way up - in the half of the flag nearest the flagpole, the wider diagonal white stripe must be above the red diagonal stripe, as Scotland's St Andrew's Cross takes precedence over Ireland's St. Patrick's Cross. It is considered improper to fly the flag upside down.

Position of Honour

Whenever any of the UK's National Flags, or any other sovereign national flags, are displayed, due consideration should be given to flag etiquette and precedence. If a purely decorative effect is desired it is better to confine the display to flags of lesser status; for example, house flags, pennants or coloured bunting.

The basic order of precedence of flags in the United Kingdom is: Royal Standards, the Union Flag, the Constituent National Flag of the home country (England, Scotland or Wales), flags of other nations (in English alphabetical order), the flag of the European Union, flags of counties, flags of cities or towns, banners of arms, and house flags. See Appendix A for a more detailed precedence list and special precedence orders for international organizations.

When the National Flags are flown with the flags of other nations each flag should have the same width (the measurement from top to bottom) and should fly from a separate flagpole of the same height. International protocol prohibits the flying of any nation's flag higher than another in peacetime (apart from medal ceremonies during sporting events). If any of the flags are square or nearly square, they can have a slightly larger width (up to 125%) to give a more equal area.

The senior National Flag (ie. the Union Flag or the Constituent National Flag of the home country) should be raised first and lowered last, unless the number of flags permits them to be raised and lowered simultaneously. Flags should be raised briskly and lowered ceremoniously. An alternative British tradition for flag raising is to hoist the flag while still rolled up and tied with a thin piece of cotton or a slip knot. A sharp tug of the halyard will break the cotton and release the flag to fly free. This is known as 'breaking' the flag, and is often used to mark the beginning of an event, or the arrival of a VIP.

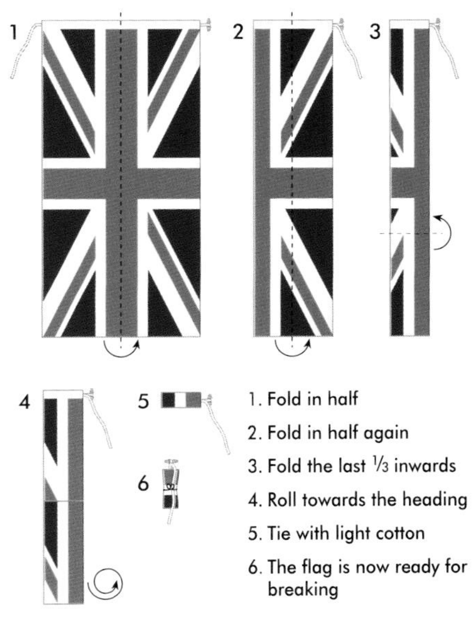

1
2
3
4
5
6
1. Fold in half
2. Fold in half again
3. Fold the last ⅓ inwards
4. Roll towards the heading
5. Tie with light cotton
6. The flag is now ready for breaking

Folding a Flag for Breaking

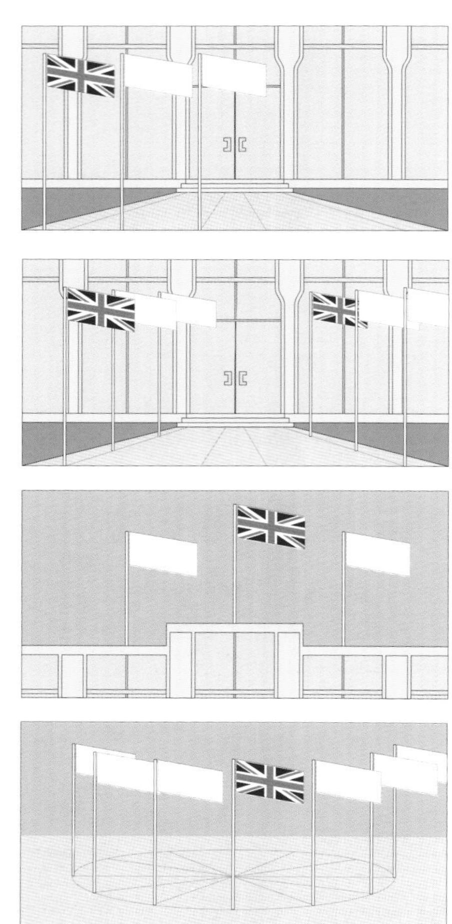

The National Flags should be displayed as follows:

On Buildings

Where there are two or more flagpoles parallel to the building line, the senior National Flag should be the first flag on the left of an observer facing the main entrance of the building. The remaining flags then appear in order of precedence from left to right.

Where there are two or more flagpoles on the forecourt of a building but at an angle to the main entrance, the senior National Flag should be flown on the outermost pole when the flagpoles are situated to the left of the main entrance and on the innermost pole when the flagpoles are to the right of the main entrance.

If only one flag is to be flown and there are two flagpoles, it should be flown on the flagpole to the observer's left. If there are more than two flagpoles, it should be flown as near as possible to the centre. This only applies when the other flagpoles remain empty.

If one flagpole is higher than the rest, then the senior National Flag can fly from that flagpole but no other national flags can be flown on the other flagpoles. These can still be used for more junior flags such as county and house flags. Alternatively the higher flagpole can be left empty and the remaining flagpoles used as if it did not exist. In general when siting flagpoles it is a good idea to keep them all at the same level to avoid these protocol problems.

The appropriate size of flag for any flagpole is a matter of aesthetics but, as a guide, a ground-level flagpole should have a flag whose length is approximately ⅓ of the pole's height. A flagpole on top of a building will need a larger flag because of the added height of the building, with a length up to ¾ of the pole's height.

Within a Circle of Flags

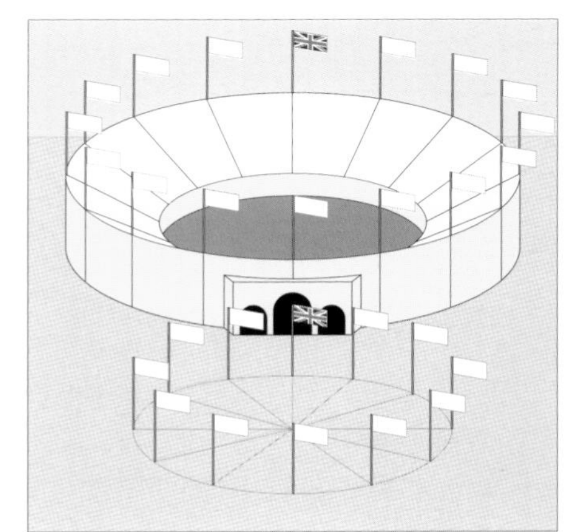

In a semi-circle of flags representing a number of nations, the senior National Flag should be in the centre. The remaining flags should be placed with the next most senior flag (or first in alphabetical order if all the flags are of equal seniority) on the left of the central flag, the next on the right of the central flag, the next on the 2nd left from the central flag, and continuing to alternate left and right.

In an enclosed circle of flags representing a number of nations, the senior National Flag should be flown on the flagpole immediately opposite the main entrance to the venue, or above the Royal Box if there is no main entrance. The remaining flags should be arranged as for the semi-circle of flags described above.

From a Flagpole with Yardarm and Gaff

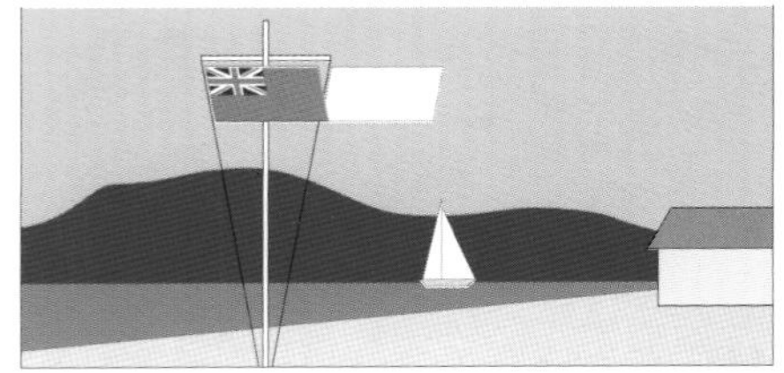

When displayed with the flag of another nation on a flagpole fitted with yard-arms (horizontal cross-pieces), the senior National Flag should be positioned on the left yardarm as viewed from the front.

If the flagpole is fitted with a gaff (a short pole attached to the flagpole at an angle - see illustration), the senior National Flag, normally in this case an ensign, should be flown from the gaff. If another national flag is to be flown on the same flagpole it can be flown from a yardarm as described above.

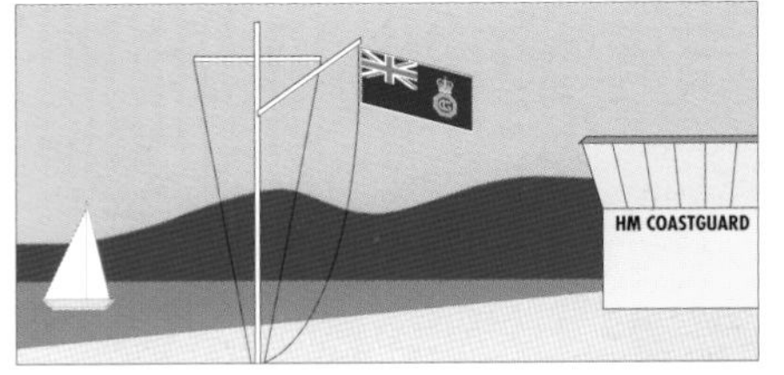

A yacht club burgee or distinguishing flag can be flown from the peak, the highest point of the flagpole, without breaching protocol.

In Processions

The senior National Flag should always lead in a single file of flags.

When two or more flags are carried side-by-side, the senior National Flag takes the position of honour on the right-hand end of the line facing the direction of movement.

When passing the person taking the salute the flag should be lowered so that the staff is horizontal or almost horizontal. This can be done by simply lowering the staff straight ahead, or by lowering the staff towards the person taking the salute and then swinging it round to be straight ahead. All the movements should be slow and graceful and care should be taken that the flag does not touch the ground. After the person taking the salute has been passed, the flag should be raised to its original position.

With Crossed Flags

Whenever crossed with the flag of another nation or organization, the senior National Flag should be on the left of the observer facing the flag. Its staff should be in front of the staff of the other flag.

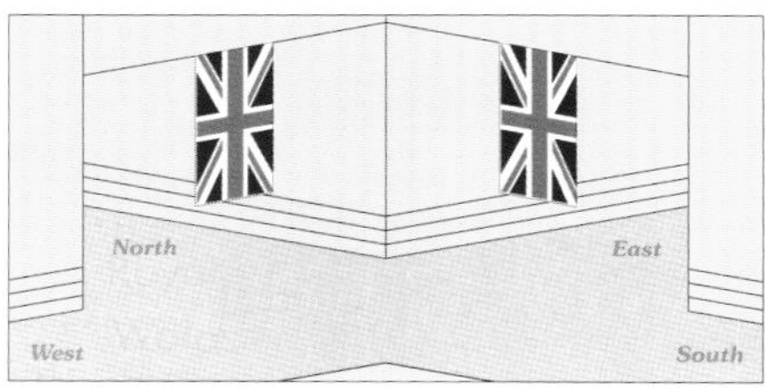

Suspended Vertically Above a Street

The flag's top-left corner (the canton), or uppermost broad white diagonal in the case of the Union Flag, should be on the north side in an east-west street, and the east side in a north-south street, thus being on the left of the observer facing east or south respectively.

Flat Against a Surface

Union Flag - If hung horizontally or vertically, the uppermost broad white diagonal should be in the top-left corner.

Other flags - If hung vertically, the edge that would normally be the top of the flag should be on the left, so, for example, ensigns have their Union Flag canton in the upper left corner. On ensigns that have an armorial badge, if possible the badge should be upright, and the correct way round.

On a Speaker's Platform

When displayed from a staff, on a speaker's platform, the senior National Flag should be placed on the right-hand side of the speaker. For interior or parade use a "Dress Flag" may be used. This is normally made of silk or satin with a fringe around three sides. The fringe can be gold or red/white/blue for the Union Flag, red/white for St. George's Cross, blue/white for St. Andrew's Cross and green/white for the Red Dragon. The fringe is purely decorative.

As a Pall for a Casket at Funerals

If one of the National Flags is to be placed on a coffin during a funeral procession or service, it should be placed so that the top-left corner of the flag is over the deceased's left shoulder. The flag should be removed before interment or cremation and folded.

In the United Kingdom it is not normal practice to present the flag to the next of kin, but should they have expressed a desire to retain the flag it may be presented to them after being folded. There is no prescribed method of folding the flag for this purpose, and any method that produces the desired result can be used.

On Vehicles

If a vehicle is to fly a car flag it should be placed on a mast fitted to the front-right wing or fender, or in the centre of the front edge of the roof. If two flags are to be flown, the more senior flag should be on the front-right wing or fender and the junior flag on the front-left wing or fender.

When flags are painted onto a vehicle, for example on the tail fin of an aircraft, the flag on the port side should show the obverse of the flag (ie. the flagpole on the left), while that on the starboard side should show the reverse (ie. the flagpole on the right). On surfaces perpendicular to the direction of travel the obverse of the flag should be shown.

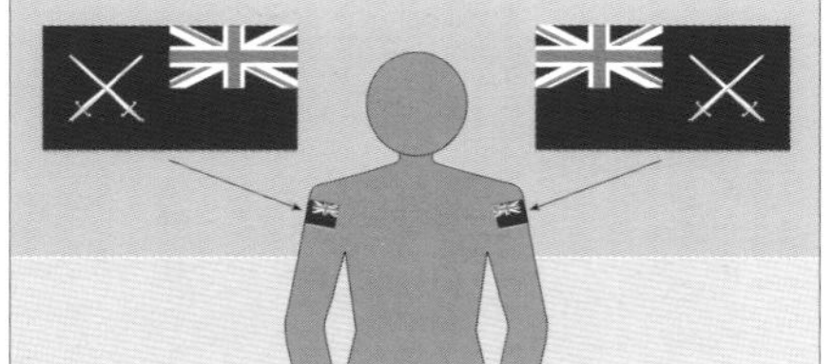

On Uniforms

When flag shoulder patches are used on uniforms the flag on the left shoulder or sleeve should show the obverse of the flag (ie. the flagpole at the wearer's front). If it is considered necessary to have a patch on the right shoulder or sleeve it should show the reverse of the flag (ie. still with the flagpole at the wearer's front). If more than one flag is to be shown, the Union Flag should be at the top.

The Civil Air Ensign

At Civilian Transport Facilities

Civilian marine facilities should fly the Civil Ensign (the Red Ensign) as their national flag, unless they belong to an organization that holds a warrant for a special ensign, when that ensign should be used instead.

Civilian air facilities, such as airports and airfields, should fly the Civil Air Ensign as their national flag, rather than the Union Flag. They may additionally fly the appropriate constituent national flag.

At International Sporting Events

The protocol for flags at international sporting events is slightly different. In some cases, such as the Olympic and Commonwealth Games the flag of the International Olympic Committee or Commonwealth Games Federation takes precedence over national flags. The flags of the various sports governing bodies also come before the national flags. It is also permitted to fly the flags of the winning nations at different heights to show who won gold, silver and bronze.

International Olympic Committee

Commonwealth Games Federation

Flags on Government Buildings

The following is a list of the days on which Her Majesty has commanded that Government buildings, including those of the National Executives and British Overseas Missions, should fly the Union Flag. Apart from in Northern Ireland (where flag flying is limited by the *Flags Regulations [Northern Ireland] 2000*) this does not prevent them flying the National Flags on any other day that they feel is appropriate or desirable. National Executive buildings may fly their appropriate National Flag on its own, or with the Union Flag in a senior position.

20th January	Birthday of HRH The Countess of Wessex
6th February	Anniversary of Her Majesty's Accession
19th February	Birthday of HRH The Duke of York
1st March	St. David's Day (Wales and overseas only, see note 2)
10th March	Birthday of HRH The Earl of Wessex
17th March	St. Patrick's Day (Northern Ireland Civil Service buildings only)
March	Commonwealth Day (second Monday)

Two British National Flags
(see note 2)

21st April	Birthday of Her Majesty The Queen
23rd April	St. George's Day (England and overseas only, see note 2)
9th May	Europe Day (see note 3)
2nd June	Anniversary of Coronation Day
10th June	Birthday of HRH The Duke of Edinburgh
June	Official Celebration of Her Majesty's Birthday (announced annually)
15th August	Birthday of HRH The Princess Royal
November	Remembrance Day (second Sunday, see note 4)
14th November	Birthday of HRH The Prince of Wales and Duke of Rothesay
20th November	Anniversary of Her Majesty's Wedding
30th November	St. Andrew's Day (Scotland and overseas only, see note 2)

In the Greater London area on the day of the Opening and Prorogation of a Session of the United Kingdom Parliament. In Scotland, Wales and Northern Ireland on the day of the Opening and Prorogation of a Session of their Parliament or Assembly, normally only in the appropriate capital, unless the Parliament or Assembly is sitting in another city (see note 2).

Notes:

1. The defaced Union Flags (ie. those of Governors, Commissioners, Ambassadors, High Commissioners, Consuls and Lord Lieutenants) and *appropriate* ensigns, ie. the White Ensign, the RAF Ensign, the Red Ensign and the defaced Blue Ensigns may fly in place of the Union Flag.
2. Where a building, including a British Overseas Mission, has two or more flagpoles the appropriate National Flag may be flown in addition to the Union Flag but not in a senior position. If there is only one flagpole the appropriate National Flag may be

flown under the Union Flag, with a gap of about 30cm, assuming there is enough vertical space on the pole. When flags are at half-mast the lower flag must be removed.

3. The Union Flag should fly alongside the European Flag, in the senior position. On Government buildings that only have one flagpole, the Union Flag should take precedence.
4. Flags should be flown at full-mast all day.
5. The Royal Standard is never hoisted when the Royal person is passing in procession. If the Royal person is to be present in a building, the Lord Chamberlain's Department, Buckingham Palace, London SW1 should be consulted. The Standard should only be flown whilst the Royal person is on the premises, being hoisted (or broken) on their arrival and lowered following their departure.

Flags at Half-mast

Half-mast means the flag is flown two-thirds of the way up the flagpole, with at least the height of the flag between the top of the flag and the top of the flagpole. On poles that are more than 45° from the vertical, flags cannot be flown at half-mast and the pole should be left empty.

When a flag is to be flown at half-mast, it should first be raised all the way to the top of the mast, allowed to remain there for a second and then be lowered to the half-mast position. When it is being lowered from half-mast, it should again be raised to the top of the mast for a second before being fully lowered.

When one of the National Flags is at half-mast, other flags on the same stand of poles should also be at half-mast or should not be flown at all. Flags of foreign nations should not be flown, unless their country is also observing mourning.

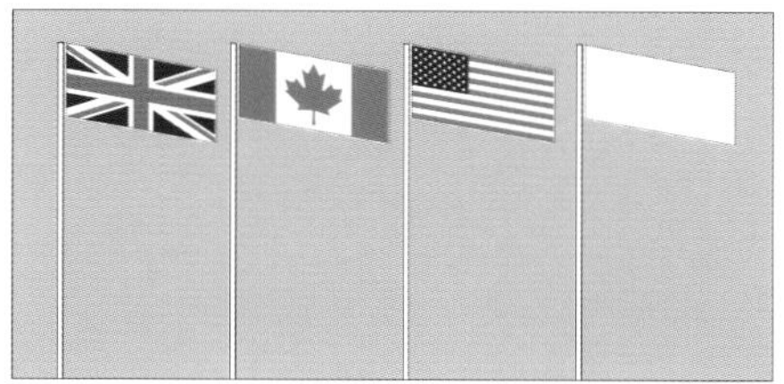

A Stand of Flags at Full-mast

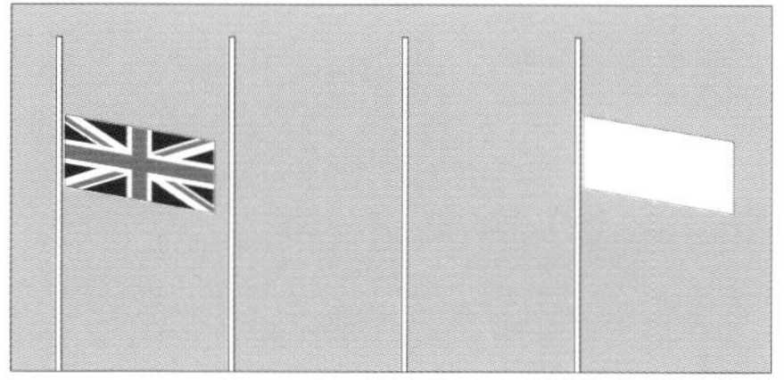

The Same Stand at Half-mast

The Royal Standard never flies at half-mast. It represents the Monarchy, which is continuous, and it would therefore be inappropriate for it to fly at half-mast.

Flags should be flown at half-mast on the following occasions:

a. From the announcement of the death until the funeral of the Sovereign, except on Proclamation Day when flags are flown right up following the proclamation.
b. From the announcement of the death until the funeral of a member of the Royal Family styled 'Royal Highness', subject to special commands from Her Majesty in each case.
c. On the day of the announcement of the death and on the day of the funeral of other members of the Royal Family, subject to special commands from Her Majesty in each case.
d. The funerals of foreign Rulers, subject to special commands from Her Majesty in each case.
e. The funerals of Prime Ministers and ex-Prime Ministers of the United Kingdom, subject to special commands from Her Majesty in each case.
f. The funerals of First Ministers and ex-First Ministers of Scotland, Wales and Northern Ireland, subject to special commands from Her Majesty in each case. Unless otherwise commanded by Her Majesty, this only applies to flags in their respective countries.
g. At British Embassies, High Commissions and Missions when flags in the host country are being flown at half-mast, subject to the discretion of the *Chef de Mission*.
h. Any other occasions where Her Majesty has given a special command.

If a Flag Day occurs on a day when flags are flying at half-mast, the flags should still be flown at half-mast.

If the body of a very distinguished subject is lying in a building, the flag should fly at half-mast on that building until the body has left.

The above cover Royal and National Mourning, and do not prevent the flying of flags at half-mast on private or non-Government buildings on other relevant occasions.

Pennants

It is often impractical to fly a proper flag all through the year - flags wear out, especially if they are flown in windy conditions. Bare flagpoles are a sad sight. The pennant, or vimpel, is a solution to these problems. The long narrow streamer-like flags are designed to be practical. The optional single point attachment and the narrow tail reduce wear and their length means that they can be easily repaired. They can be flown 24 hours a day without special lighting.

Union

England

Scotland

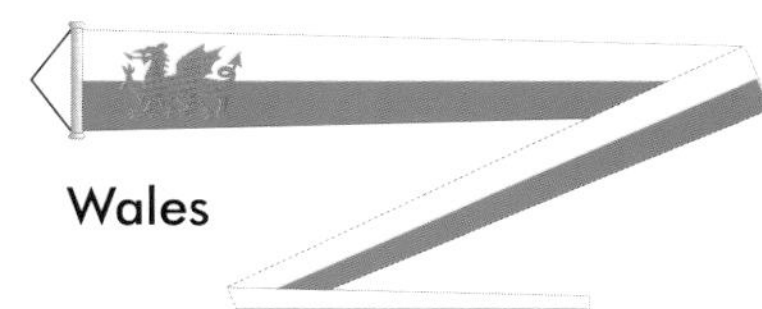
Wales

Using Flags on Items

While it is not illegal to place the National Flags on items such as teacloths or underwear, it is strongly discouraged. If any of the National Flags is used on items it should not be defaced by any other text or symbol and should be treated with respect.

The Proper Disposal of Flags

When a flag becomes tattered or faded and is no longer in a suitable condition for use, it should be destroyed in a dignified way, for example by burning it privately, or by tearing or cutting it into strips that no longer resemble the original flag.

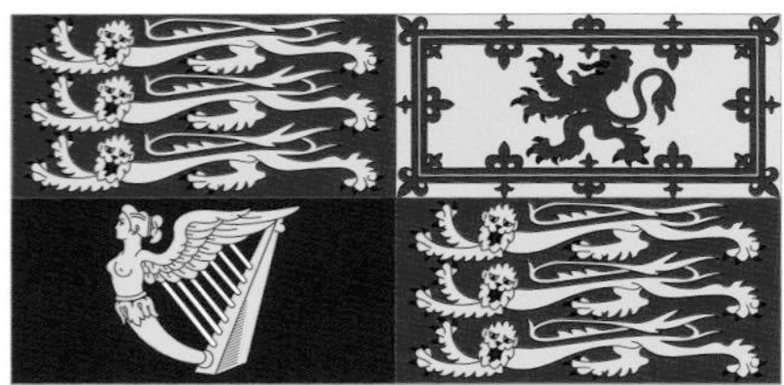

The Royal Standard for use in England, Wales & Northern Ireland

The Royal Standard for use in Scotland

Personal Flag of HM The Queen

The Royal Standard or Banner

The elements of the Royal Standard date back several centuries:

The three gold lions *passant guardant* on red are the ancient Royal Arms of England. Their first recorded use by an English monarch is by Richard I on his second Great Seal in about 1198, but they may have been used before this date. From 1337 until 1801 the Royal Arms of England were quartered with those of France (gold fleur-de-lys on blue) as the English monarchs claimed that country.

The red lion *rampant* on gold, with a double red border decorated with fleur-de-lys, is the ancient emblem of the Kings and Queens of Scots. It dates back to Alexander II (1214-1249), or possibly his father William the Lion. James VI and I quartered the English and Scottish Royal Arms when he became King of England in 1603.

The gold harp with silver strings on blue was chosen as the emblem of Ireland by Henry VIII but was not incorporated into the Royal Arms until 1603.

The form of Royal Arms used today dates back to 1837 when Queen Victoria came to the throne. The Royal Standard is a banner-of-arms, ie. the emblems on the shield are reproduced in cloth, showing the arms of England in the first and fourth quarters, those of Scotland in the second and of Ireland in the third.

There is a separate Royal Standard for use in Scotland which has Scotland in the first and fourth quarters, England in the second and Ireland in the third.

The Queen has a personal flag which is used when she visits Commonwealth countries of which she is not Head of State.

For those Commonwealth countries of which Her Majesty is Head of State there are separate personal flags, based on the Arms of each dominion, with a blue circle in the centre, bearing the Royal monogram within a chaplet of roses.

HM The Queen's Personal Flag for Australia

HM The Queen's Personal Flag for Jamaica

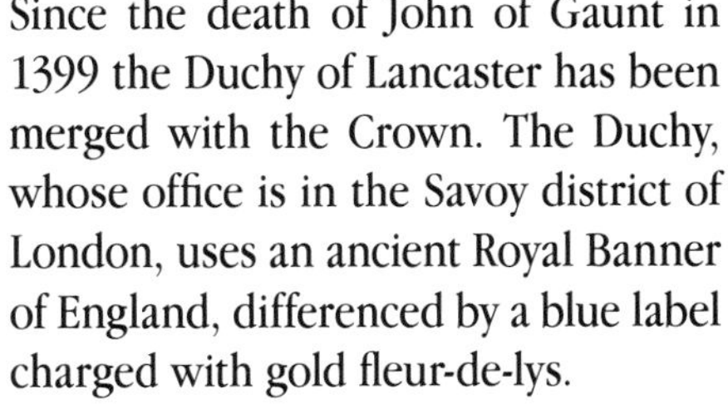

Since the death of John of Gaunt in 1399 the Duchy of Lancaster has been merged with the Crown. The Duchy, whose office is in the Savoy district of London, uses an ancient Royal Banner of England, differenced by a blue label charged with gold fleur-de-lys.

HM The Queen's Personal Flag for Barbados

HM The Queen's Personal Flag for New Zealand

The Duchy of Lancaster

HM The Queen's Personal Flag for Canada

The Ancient Scottish Royal Standard

The Ancient Scottish Royal Standard

The usage of the Lion Rampant banner follows Scottish practice in that it is not restricted to the monarch but is used by the monarch's high-ranking representatives. These are the Lord High Commissioner to the General Assembly of the Church of Scotland, the Lord Lyon King of Arms, the Keeper of the Great Seal (who is the Scottish First Minister) and the Lord Lieutenants of the Counties.

In 1934, as part of the preparations for his Silver Jubilee, King George V issued a Royal Warrant granting the Scots permission to use the Lion Rampant as a sign of loyalty and celebration. The warrant does not permit a person or organization to fly the flag from a flagpole - that would be an offence against Scottish heraldic law - but it does allow for the flag to be waved by hand. So, for example, Scottish sports fans have two different flags to use, the St. Andrew's Cross and the Lion Rampant.

Other Members of the Royal Family

The other members of the Royal Family also have personal standards. Most of these follow the traditional heraldic pattern of adding a white label with appropriate emblems to the Royal Standard; for example the Duke of York uses a blue anchor, Prince William uses a red scallop shell and the Princess Royal uses two crosses and a heart, all in red. Children of a sovereign have three white label points, while grandchildren have five, apart from the second heir apparent. The standard of HRH The Duke of Edinburgh shows the arms of Denmark, Greece, Mountbatten and Edinburgh. There is an "Other Members" standard for those who do not have standards, eg. the wives of the Royal Dukes and Princes.

HRH The Duke of Edinburgh

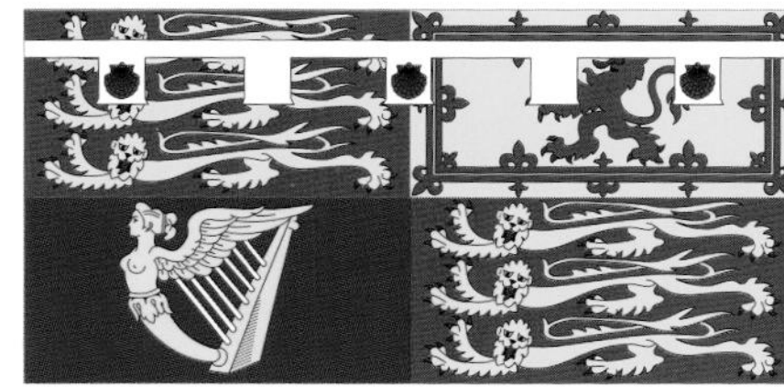
HRH Prince Henry "Harry" of Wales

HRH The Princess Royal

HRH The Prince of Wales
(not in Scotland or Wales)

HRH The Duke of York

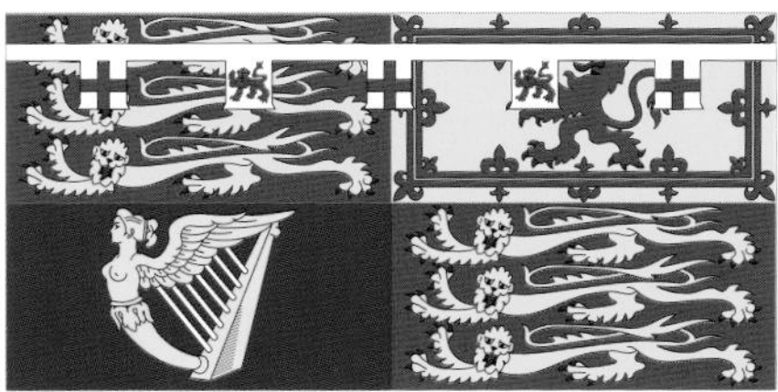
HRH The Duke of Gloucester

HRH Prince William of Wales

HRH The Earl of Wessex

HRH The Duke of Kent

HRH Prince Michael of Kent

HRH Princess Alexandra

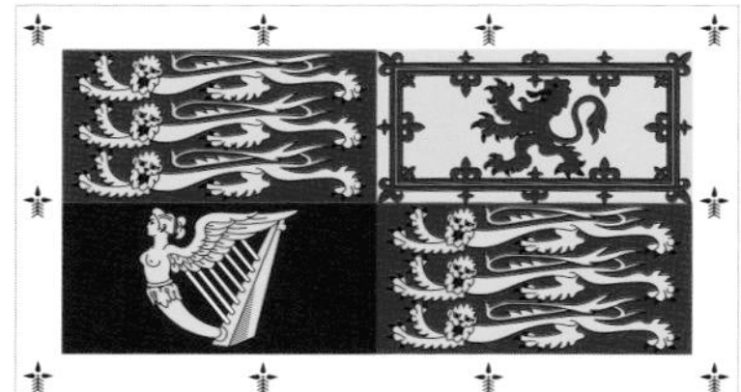

The Other Members' Standard

HRH The Prince of Wales has separate standards for use in Wales and Cornwall.

His Welsh standard shows the arms of Wales (based on those of Llelwyn, the last Welsh Prince of Wales), with an escutcheon containing a prince's coronet. The coronet has only one arch, rather than the two of a full crown. The four lions appear as an escutcheon, ensigned by the Prince's coronet on his standard for use in England and Northern Ireland.

As Duke of Cornwall his Cornish standard shows the ancient arms of the Duchy of Cornwall, black with fifteen bezants, or gold balls.

The Prince of Wales has a Royal Badge of three ostrich plumes with the motto "*Ich Dien*" (I Serve). This badge has been used by the heir apparent since Edward, The Black Prince, son of Edward III. The feathers probably come from the family of his mother, Philippa of Hainault, whose own father was Lord of Ostrevans.

HRH The Prince of Wales
in Wales

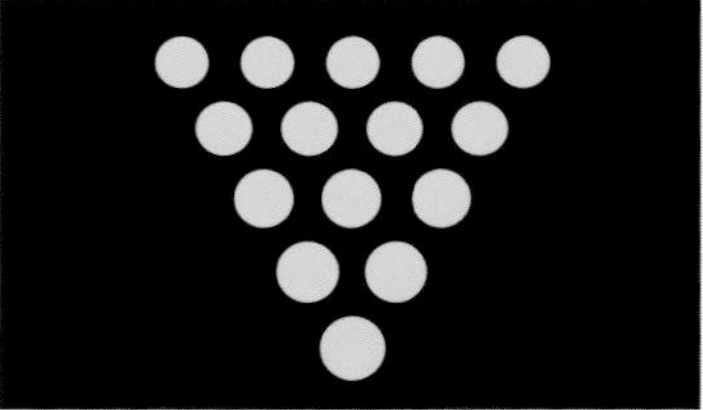

HRH The Duke of Cornwall
(Prince Charles' Cornish title)

"The Prince of Wales' Feathers"
Badge of the heir apparent

Senior members of the Royal Family have matriculated Scottish personal arms that use the Scottish quartering of the Royal Arms. HRH The Duke of Rothesay, Prince Charles' Scottish title, has a personal standard that quarters the arms of the Great Steward of Scotland and the Lord of the Isles with an escutcheon of the arms of the Duke of Rothesay and Prince of Scotland. HRH The Duke of Edinburgh's standard is the same in both Kingdoms. The Duke of York, Earl of Wessex and the Princess Royal have the same labels differencing their arms as they do elsewhere.

HRH The Duke of Rothesay
(Prince Charles' Scottish title)

HRH The Princess Royal
in Scotland

HRH The Duke of York
in Scotland

HRH The Earl of Wessex
in Scotland

The Royal Cypher for use in England, Wales & Northern Ireland

The Royal Arms and Cypher

There are two versions of the Royal Arms. The first shows a golden helm with a crest of a lion *statant guardant* on a St. Edward's crown - this is for the personal use of HM The Queen. The second version omits the helmet and crest which are replaced with a St. Edward's crown - these are the arms of HM The Queen as Head of State, or State Arms, and are used by HM Government. There is also a Royal Cypher which appears on ceremonial uniforms, is used by the Royal Mail and appears on various other items, such as the red dispatch boxes of Government Ministers. ER stands for the Latin *Elizabeth Regina* (Elizabeth The Queen).

The Royal Arms for use in England, Wales & Northern Ireland

The Royal Arms as used by HM Government

The Royal Arms as used by HM Government Black & White Version

The Scottish Royal Arms and Cypher

Scotland has its own Royal Regalia and heraldic law, administered by the Lord Lyon King of Arms. The Scottish crown has no pearls on its arches and different emblems on the rim of the coronet. It is used wherever the St. Edward's crown would be used elsewhere in the United Kingdom, for example in the Royal Cypher. The Royal Arms for use in Scotland have the supporters reversed, have a collar and badge of the Order of the Thistle around the shield and a crest of a seated lion holding a sword and a sceptre.

The Royal Cypher
for use in Scotland

The Royal Arms for use in Scotland

The Royal Arms
as used by the Scottish Executive
and HM Government in Scotland

The Royal Arms
as used by the Scottish Executive
Black & White Version

The Ministry of Defence Emblem

Ministry of Defence

Flags of the Armed Forces

The modern use of flags originated with the military. Early armies carried standards or vexilloids (a staff with an emblem at the top) into battle as a rallying point. In fact the modern name for the study of flags, vexillology, is derived from the Latin *vexillum*, the small square of cloth hanging from a cross-bar on a staff that Roman legions carried into battle.

Mediæval Italian city states, such as Genoa, started using flags to differentiate their ships in the 12th century, creating the modern 'national' flag. Incidentally the flag of Genoa is white with a red St. George's Cross, the same as the modern flag of England. Britain's national flag, the Union Flag, is originally a maritime flag whose use has become more general over the centuries.

For much of the last millennium military flags were heraldic in nature, often including elements from the officers' coat-of-arms. In modern times they have changed to include regimental badges and national emblems rather than personal ones.

Britain has a rich set of armed forces flags, from flags to identify the different services, distinguishing flags for the senior ranks in each service, flags to indicate the holders of various appointments and commands, through to the beautifully embroidered Colours used on ceremonial occasions. The use of all these flags is governed by Queen's Regulations for the Royal Navy, Army and Royal Air Force, the rules that govern all aspects of military life.

Joint Services

Joint Service flags combine the colours of the three services, dark blue for the Royal Navy, red for the Army and sky blue for the Royal Air Force. They feature the badge of the Ministry of Defence in various forms. Although several of them look like ensigns, they are distinguishing flags.

Joint Service Flag

Secretary of State for Defence

Joint Commander-in-Chief

Joint Commander 2 Star

Chief of the Defence Staff

Joint Commander 3 Star

Joint Commander 1 Star

The White Ensign
Britain's Naval Ensign

The Royal Navy

The Royal Navy is Britain's senior service. In the 17th century the Royal Navy was organized by squadrons: the red, the white and the blue, each identified by appropriately coloured ensigns. After 1702 a St. George's Cross was added to the White Ensign to avoid its being confused with the then flag of France. Since 1864, when the squadronal system ended, all commissioned ships in the Royal Navy have flown the White Ensign.

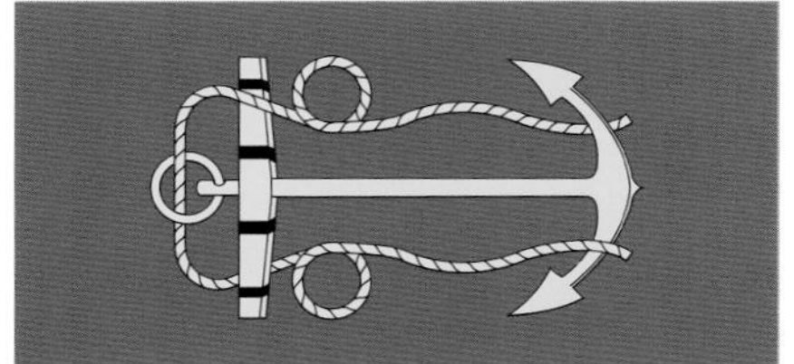

Lord High Admiral
(Her Majesty The Queen)

Navy Board

Admiral

Admiralty Board

Naval Jack, Courts Martial, Admiral of the Fleet,
1st Sea Lord, Chief of the Defence Staff (if RN)

Vice Admiral

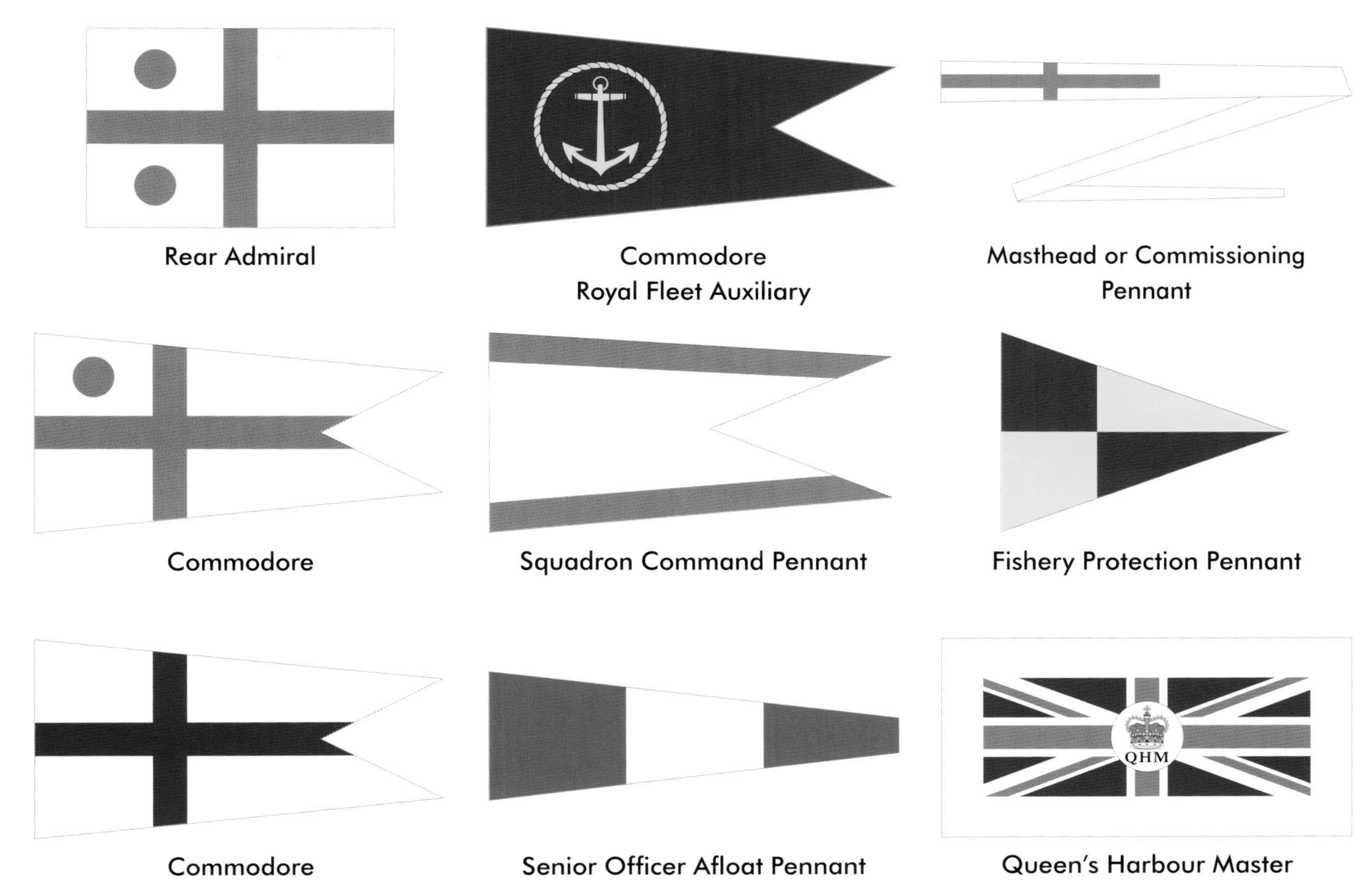

Rear Admiral

Commodore
Royal Fleet Auxiliary

Masthead or Commissioning Pennant

Commodore

Squadron Command Pennant

Fishery Protection Pennant

Commodore
Royal Naval Reserve

Senior Officer Afloat Pennant

Queen's Harbour Master

Some of the following flags are not strictly Royal Navy flags but belong to organizations which are closely associated with the Royal Navy, such as the Royal Fleet Auxiliary which provides support services to the Royal Navy around the world.

Royal Fleet Auxiliary Ensign

Royal Fleet Auxiliary Jack

Special Boat Service (SBS)
The Royal Navy's Special Forces

Royal Maritime Auxiliary Service Ensign

Royal Maritime Auxiliary Service Jack

Royal Naval Supply & Transport Service

Government Service Ensign
(also RN ships undergoing contractor's sea trials)

Government Service Jack

On occasions ships of the Royal Navy are assigned to NATO (North Atlantic Treaty Organization) or UN (United Nations) duties. At such times they usually fly the NATO or UN flag from the yardarm. They continue to wear their national colours.

The Commodore of a multi-national NATO naval force has a broad pennant with the NATO emblem in the centre. This pennant flies in addition to any personal rank flag the officer is entitled to.

When ships are sailing in convoy, escorted by Royal Naval vessels, the Commodore of the convoy flies a white flag with a blue cross.

North Atlantic
Treaty Organization

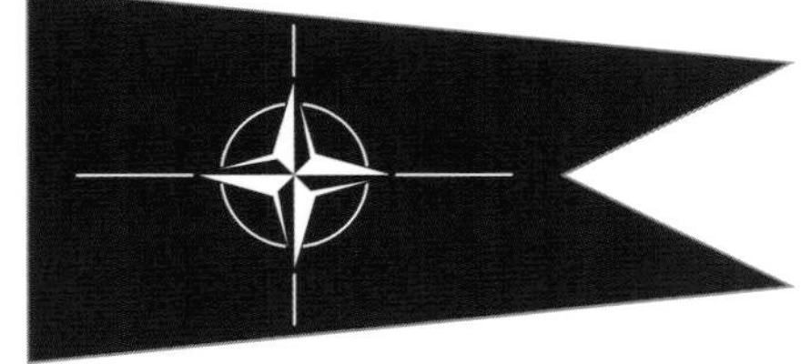

NATO Commodore

Commodore of a Convoy

United Nations

Flag Discs

The Royal Navy uses metal painted discs, about 10" in diameter, on boats to show that they are carrying an officer of flag rank who does not wish full ceremonial. Members of the Royal Family use plates with their personal emblems painted on them.

The Royal plates are equivalent to the white disc, as when full ceremonial is required the boat wears the appropriate personal standard in the bow.

Alert and Salute Only
(officer entitled to a flag)

Alert and Salute Only
(officer not entitled to a flag)

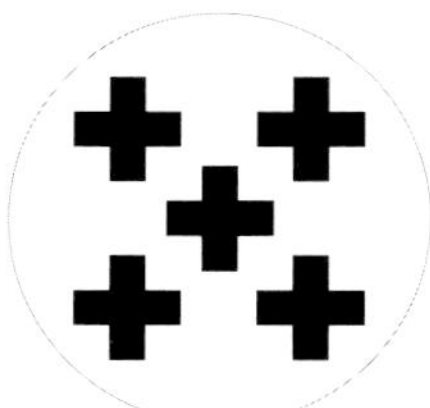

Courtesy Salute Only

HRH The Duke of Edinburgh's Plate

HRH The Prince of Wales' Plate

Royal Family Member's Plate

The Royal Marines

The Royal Marines were formed in 1664 and are the soldiers of the Royal Navy. For some 340 years they have served in the ships of the Royal Navy. During the Second World War the Commando units were formed and today make up the main force of the Royal Marines. Nearly all the Corps' flags feature the Marines' cap badge. The rank flags all show a foul anchor.

Royal Marines Corps Flag

Commandant-General Royal Marines

Major-General Royal Marines

Headquarters 3 Commando Brigade Royal Marines

General & Lieutenant-General Royal Marines

Brigadier Royal Marines

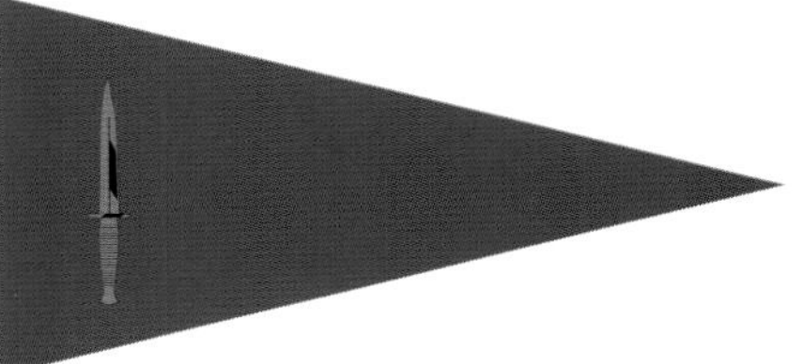

3 Commando Brigade Royal Marines Pennant

40 Commando
Royal Marines

Commando Training Centre
Royal Marines

Signals Squadron
Royal Marines

42 Commando
Royal Marines

Commando Logistics Regiment
Royal Marines

Royal Marines
School of Music

45 Commando
Royal Marines

Amphibious Trials and Training Unit
Royal Marines

Commando Helicopter Force
Royal Marines

539 Assault Squadron
Royal Marines

Royal Marines Reserve
Bristol

Royal Marines Reserve
Tyne

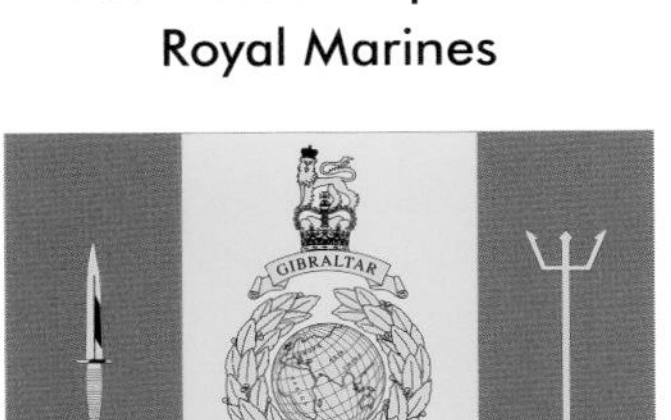

Fleet Protection Group
Royal Marines

Royal Marines Reserve
Merseyside

Royal Marines Poole

Royal Marines Reserve
City of London

Royal Marines Reserve
Scotland

The Army Flag

The British Army

The British Army is one of the oldest standing armies in the world. Some of its regiments date back to the 17th century. Regiments have Colours or Guidons (see later) and one or more Camp Flags. There is an Army Flag (or Non-ceremonial Flag), an ensign for use on vessels belonging to the Army, and many other flags, some of which are shown on the following pages.

Chief of the General Staff

General Officer Afloat
(ie. on board a ship)

Military Attaché

Field Marshal, Commander-in-Chief Forces in the Field

Army (Royal Logistics Corps) Ensign

Military Members of the Army Board

The Army uses Union Flags with a height-to-length ratio of 3:5. Ensigns are always 1:2 and the Army Flag is often also made 1:2 to match those of the other services. It also uses these appointment flags. They are usually defaced by the badge of the command.

Commander of a Corps

Brigade Commander

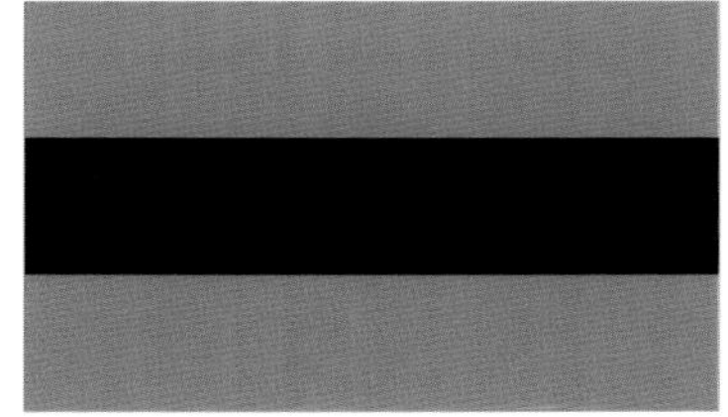

General Officer, Commander-in-Chief or Commanding a Command

Divisional Commander

Area and Sub District Commander

Senior Staff Officer on the Staff of the Commander-in-Chief

District Commander

Master Gunner
St James' Park

Camp Flags, as their name implies, are the non-ceremonial flags used to indicate the presence of a unit of a Corps or Regiment in a camp or other location. They often bear the Corps/Regimental badge in the centre, along with colours taken from the unit's shoulder patch or stable belt. The flags of different companies within a unit are usually differentiated by adding their identifying numerals or letters to the basic design.

The design of Camp Flags is up to each individual unit and as a result the designs and styles vary much more than those of the ceremonial Colours. Here is a selection of current designs :

Royal Armoured Corps
Camp Flag

The Royal Logistic Corps
Camp Flag

Royal Regiment of Artillery
Camp Flag

Corps of Royal Electrical and
Mechanical Engineers Camp Flag

Household Division
Camp Flag

Corps of Royal Engineers
Camp Flag

Army Air Corps
Camp Flag

Adjutant General's Corps
Camp Flag

Royal Army Chaplains'
Department Camp Flag

The Royal Welch Fusiliers
Camp Flag

Royal Corps of Signals
Camp Flag

1st The Queen's Dragoon Guards
Camp Flag

The Parachute Regiment
Camp Flag

Intelligence Corps
Camp Flag

The Royal Irish Regiment
Camp Flag

The Royal Gurkha Rifles
Camp Flag

The Royal Air Force Ensign

The Royal Air Force

The Royal Air Force was formed in 1918 by the merger of the Royal Flying Corps and the Royal Naval Air Service. Its ensign features the roundel that was painted onto British aircraft in 1918. Over the years the roundel on aircraft has been modified, but that on flags has not changed. The RAF has both Rank Flags (eg. Group Captain) and Appointment Flags (eg. Station Commander).

Marshal of the Royal Air Force

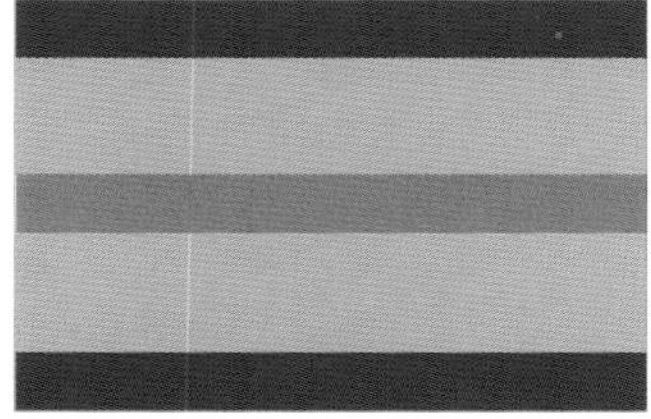
Air Marshal

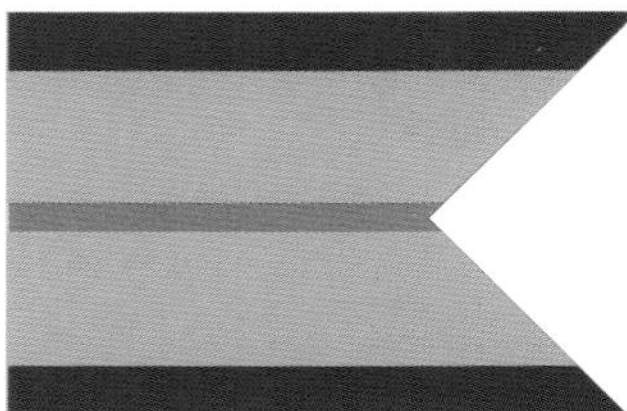
Air Commodore

Air Chief Marshal

Air Vice-Marshal

Group Captain

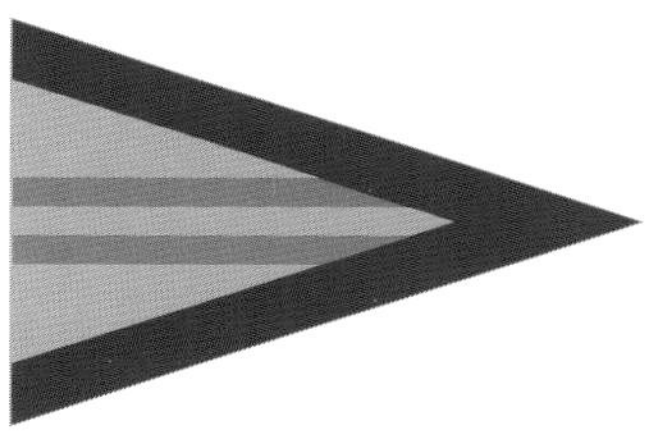

Wing Commander

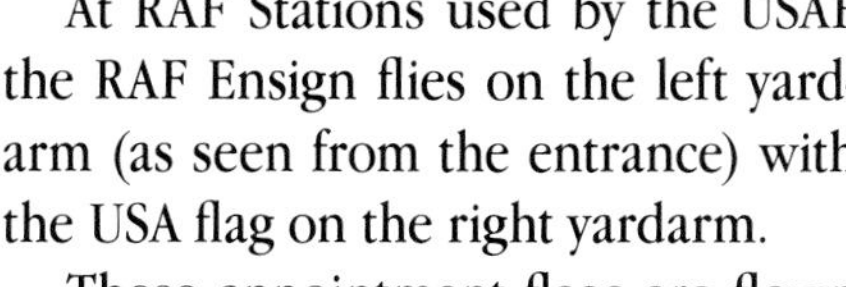

At RAF Stations used by the USAF the RAF Ensign flies on the left yardarm (as seen from the entrance) with the USA flag on the right yardarm.

These appointment flags are flown on aircraft, vessels and vehicles when the appointed officer is on board.

Air Officers Commanding-in-Chief (Commands in the UK)

Squadron Leader (in this case of No 12 Squadron)

Chief of the Air Staff, Air Attachés & Advisers, Heads of RAF Missions

Air Officers Commanding, Commandant-General RAF Regiment

The preceding Rank Flags are flown to indicate the rank of Commanding Officers at RAF Stations. The RAF Ensign is flown at the gaff/peak on RAF Stations (together with the Commanding Officer's Rank Flag at the head) or at the head/truck of a plain mast on a formation headquarters building.

RAF Members of the Air Force Board

Station Commanders

RAF Aircraft Markings

Training Aircraft Roundel

The Royal Flying Corps was created in 1912, and since 1914 British military aircraft have had red, white and blue markings to show their nationality. These are now shown in two main forms: a roundel, a device of concentric circles that appears on the main fuselage and wings; and a fin flash that appears on the tail fin. There are several different versions for various purposes, such as the low-visibility markings that are used on camouflaged combat aircraft. The roundels sometimes form part of larger markings that are specific to a particular squadron.

Non-combat Aircraft Roundel

Combat Aircraft Roundel

Low-visibility Aircraft Roundel

Non-combat Aircraft Fin Flash

Combat Aircraft Fin Flash

Low-visibility Aircraft Fin Flash

Cadet Forces

The Cadet Forces of the United Kingdom can trace their origins back to 1856 when sailors, returning from the Crimean War, established 'Naval Lads Brigades' in Whitstable and other ports.

Today they offer teenagers the opportunity to find out about life in the armed forces, with an emphasis on self-development and achievement. Most Cadet Forces offer access to The Duke of Edinburgh's Award Scheme.

There are three separate Cadet Forces for the three Services. In addition there is a Combined Cadet Force (CCF). Units of the CCF are connected with a school, and in some independent schools membership of the CCF is compulsory for at least part of a pupil's attendance at the school.

Individual units have flags in navy blue, red over blue, sky blue or green with the badge of the Cadet Force in the centre and the name of the unit or school on each side.

Sea Cadet Corps Ensign

Army Cadet Force

Combined Cadet Force

Naval Section
Combined Cadet Force Ensign

Air Training Corps

Military Colours

The Queen's Colour of The Royal Navy

"Colours" are the flags that were used on battlefields to rally the troops to their units. Today Colours are no longer used in battle, but they are still held in great honour, and are saluted by passing servicemen. The Royal Navy and Royal Naval Reserve have Queen's Colours. Commandos of Royal Marines and battalions of infantry regiments (except for The Royal Green Jackets and The Royal Gurkha Rifles) have two Colours, a Queen's Colour and a Regimental Colour. The Guards also have Company Colours and three of them have State Colours. The background of the Regimental Colours (or Queen's for the Guards) are based on the regiments' ancient uniform 'facings' colour. Artillery regiments use their artillery pieces as their Colours. Cavalry regiments mainly have Guidons, but the Life Guards and Blues and Royals have Sovereign's Standards. The Royal Air Force has Queen's Colours and Squadron Standards.

The Queen's Colour of 40 Commando, The Royal Marines

The Regimental Colour of 40 Commando, The Royal Marines

The Sovereign's Standard of The Blues and Royals

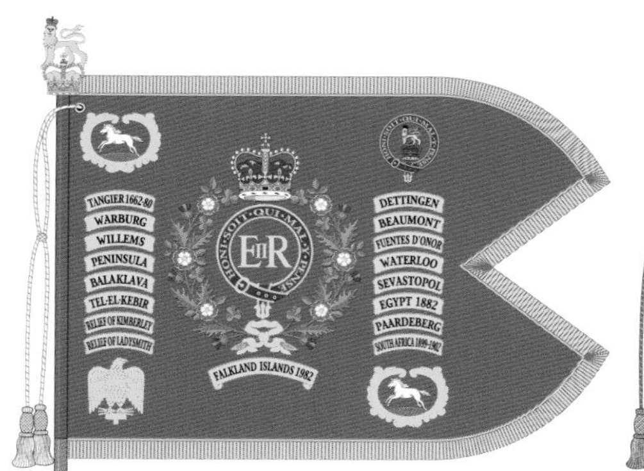

The Cavalry Guidon of
The Blues and Royals

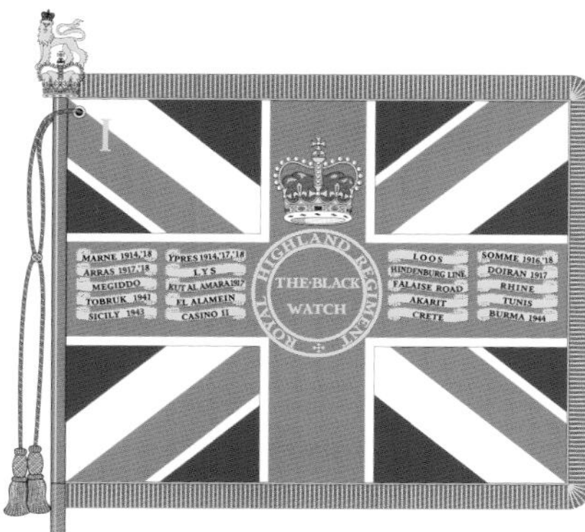

The Queen's Colour of
1st Battalion, The Black Watch

The Regimental Colour of
1st Battalion, The Black Watch

The Company Colour of No.1 Coy.,
1st Battalion, Irish Guards

The Queen's Colour for
The Royal Air Force in the UK

The Squadron Standard of
No.32 (The Royal) Squadron, RAF

Veterans' Organizations

The British Legion was founded in 1921 to provide services for ex-servicemen and women (it became the Royal British Legion in 1971). Each branch of the Legion has its own standard. These are similar to the National Standard shown here but without the badge, and with the name of the branch in blue on the gold stripe. In the branch standards the Union Flag touches the gold stripe.

The Royal Navy and RAF also have their own associations. There are associations for various other veteran groupings, such as those who served on the same ship or in the same campaign or war. The National Standard of the British Korean Veterans Association, for veterans of the Korean War, is shown as an example.

National Standard of
The Royal British Legion

National Standard of
The Royal Naval Association

National Standard of
The Royal Air Forces Association

National Standard of The British
Korean Veterans Association

Star Plates

The use of Rank Flags on cars now tends to be restricted to ceremonial usage. The more normal means of identifying a senior officer's car or vehicle is by the use of "Star Plates". These plates show the star rank of the officer (as used within many NATO forces), the background giving the branch of the forces.

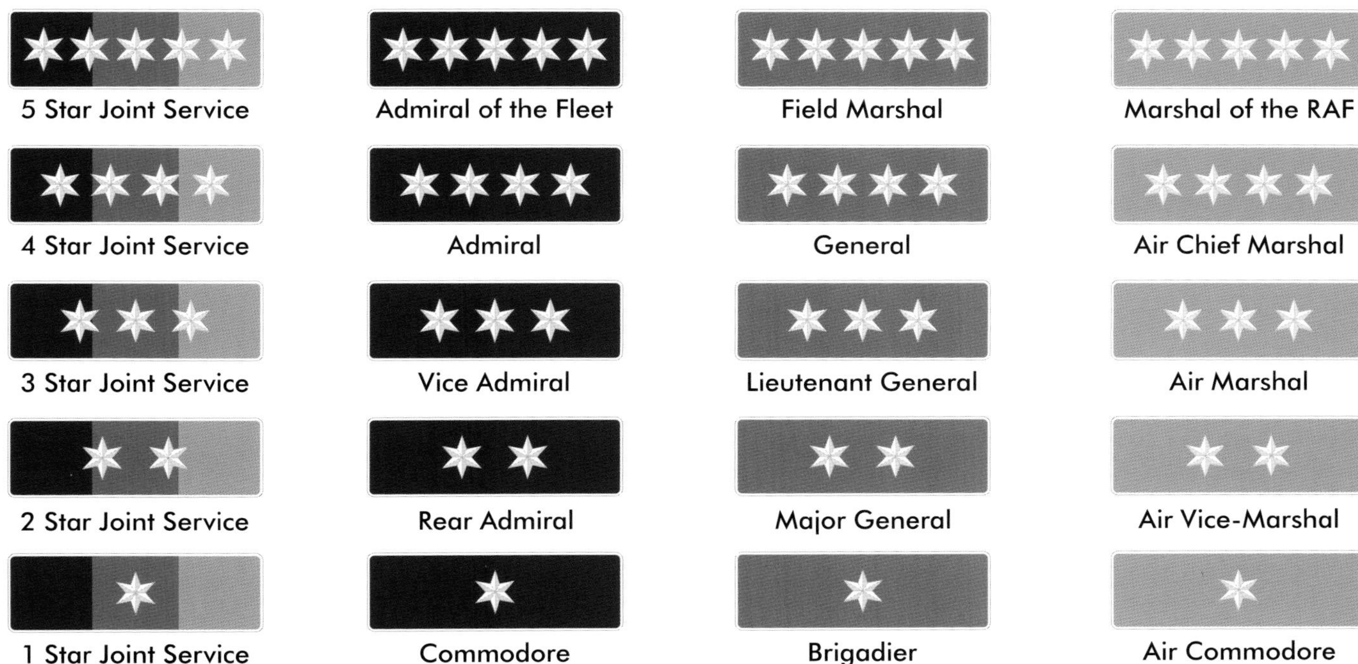

Joint Service	Navy	Army	Air Force
5 Star Joint Service	Admiral of the Fleet	Field Marshal	Marshal of the RAF
4 Star Joint Service	Admiral	General	Air Chief Marshal
3 Star Joint Service	Vice Admiral	Lieutenant General	Air Marshal
2 Star Joint Service	Rear Admiral	Major General	Air Vice-Marshal
1 Star Joint Service	Commodore	Brigadier	Air Commodore

State and Government Flags

Governors, Lieutenant Governors, Commissioners and others administering a Government (badge within the garland)

The Diplomatic Service has a set of flags for use by Governors, Commissioners, Ambassadors and Consuls. The Crown's representatives in the UK, the Lord Lieutenants, and the High Sheriffs have distinguishing flags.

HM Customs & Excise, HM Coastguard, several UK Government departments, and one Scottish Executive department, have flags, mainly for use on their vessels. Some Government agencies also have their own flags.

Diplomatic officers ashore and afloat

Consular officers afloat (not to be flown as an ensign)

Scottish Lord Lieutenants of the Counties, First Minister & Lord Lyon

Consular officers ashore

Lord Lieutenants of the Counties

High Sheriffs (England & Wales)

HM Customs & Excise Ensign

Department for the Environment, Food and Rural Affairs Ensign

Scottish Executive Department for Rural Affairs Ensign

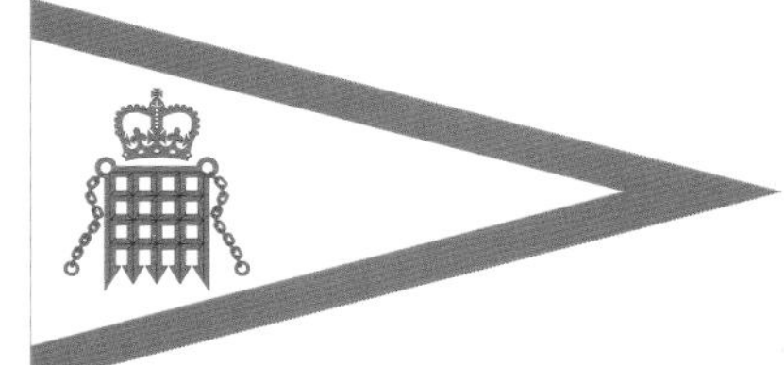
HM Customs & Excise Commissioners' Pennant

Department of Trade and Industry Ensign

Environment Agency

HM Coastguard Ensign

Department for Transport Ensign

Forestry Commission

Fire Service Flag

(The Fire Service College is used as an example)

Emergency and Rescue Services

Many of Britain's emergency and rescue services have flags of their own. The flags of Fire Services are unusual in that the field is quartered blue and red. The badge goes in the bottom blue quarter. The Metropolitan Police and the Ministry of Defence Police have defaced Blue Ensigns for use on boats. The Police Service of Northern Ireland has a single flag for all uses. The Red Cross and the St John Ambulance Brigade have flags. The Scottish St Andrew's Ambulance does not use a flag.

Metropolitan Police Ensign

Ministry of Defence Police Ensign

The Red Cross

Metropolitan Police Flag

Police Service of Northern Ireland

The St John Ambulance

Heritage Organizations

Much of Britain's natural and architectural heritage is protected by the National Trust and the National Trust for Scotland. Both these organizations have flags, although they also often use the flags of the families who originally owned the properties.

Four organizations are responsible for the upkeep and preservation of historic monuments and buildings owned by the state. They each have a simple flag that is flown from their properties.

National Trust

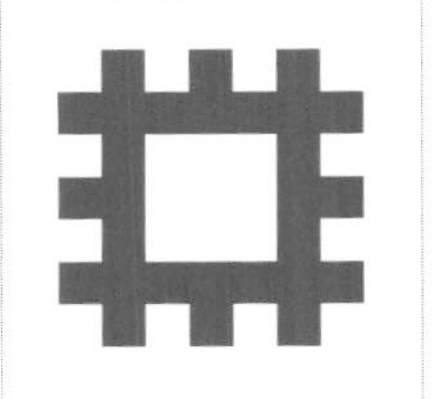

English Heritage

Cadw
(Wales)

National Trust for Scotland

Historic Scotland

Environment and Heritage Service
(Northern Ireland)

Angus

Regions and Counties

Each country in the UK is made up of counties. Most county councils have a flag. Unfortunately many of these are just logos on a plain background. The selection shown here are either the traditional flag for a region or county, or a banner of the arms of the county. The banners of arms are technically the sole property of the council, but are often used by the people of the county by tradition, and sometimes with the specific permission of the council.

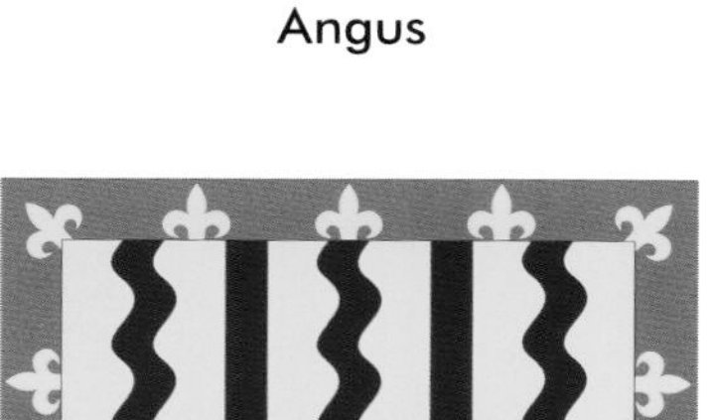
Cambridgeshire

Derbyshire

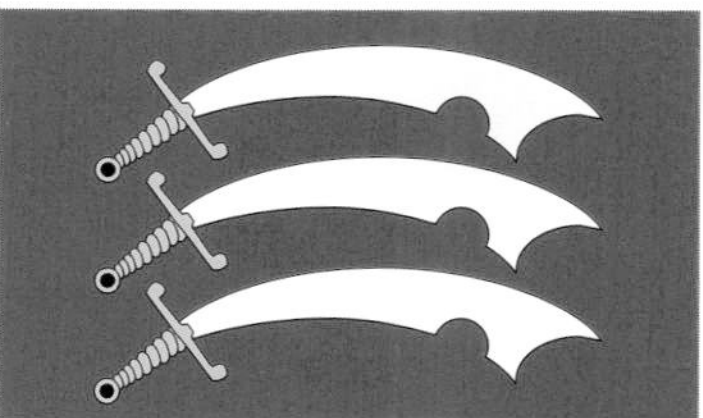
Essex

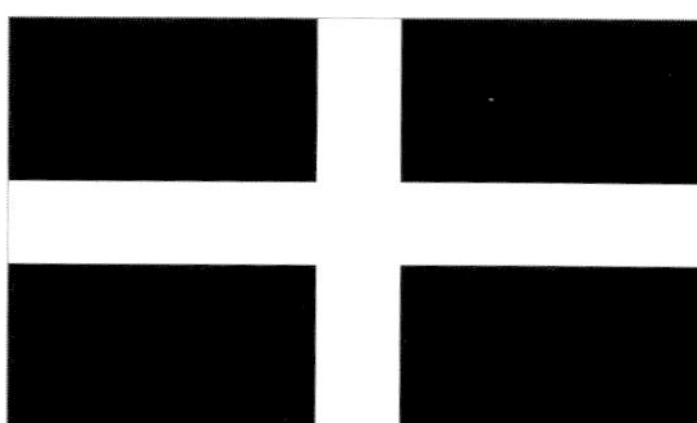
Cornwall - St. Pirran's Cross

East Anglia Region

Hampshire

Kent

Northumberland

Rutland

Lancashire

Orkney Islands

Shetland Islands

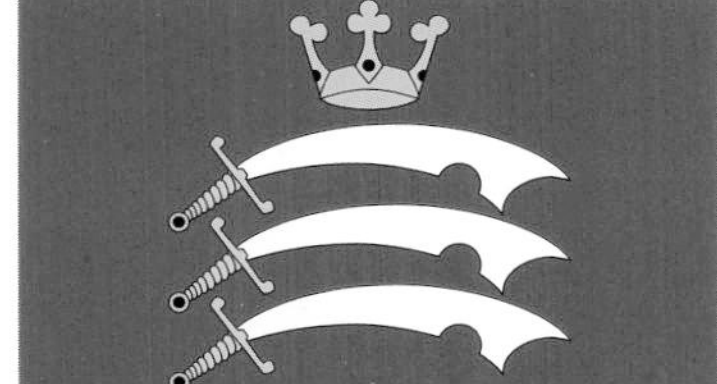
Middlesex

Pembrokeshire

County Tyrone

Aberdeen

Cities and Towns

All the cities, and most of the towns, in the UK have coats-of-arms, and many of them use banners of these arms on their civic buildings and on the official car of their Mayor, Provost, Lord Mayor or Lord Provost. As with the armorial county flags they are technically for the sole use of the city or town's council, but in some cases they are used more widely. Many councils also use their logo as a basis for a flag.

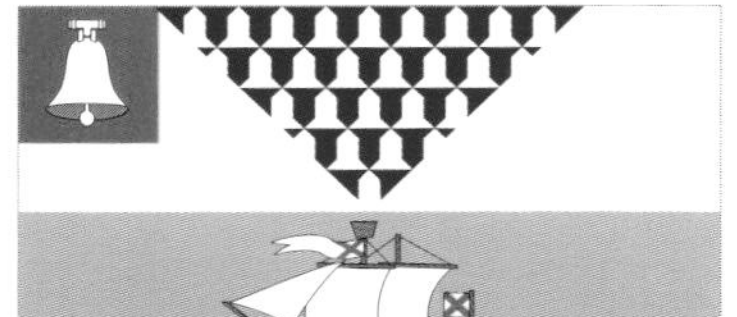
Belfast

Cardiff

Edinburgh

Birmingham

Durham

Lincoln

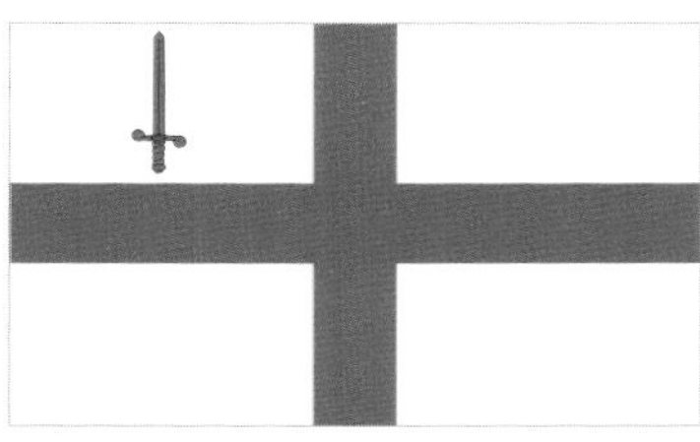

City of London

St Albans

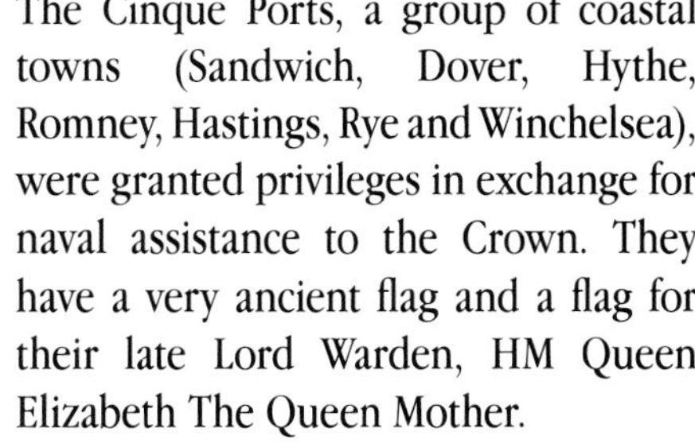

The Cinque Ports, a group of coastal towns (Sandwich, Dover, Hythe, Romney, Hastings, Rye and Winchelsea), were granted privileges in exchange for naval assistance to the Crown. They have a very ancient flag and a flag for their late Lord Warden, HM Queen Elizabeth The Queen Mother.

Lord Mayor of London

Stirling

Cinque Ports

Portsmouth

York

Lord Warden of the Cinque Ports
(HM Queen Elizabeth The Queen Mother)

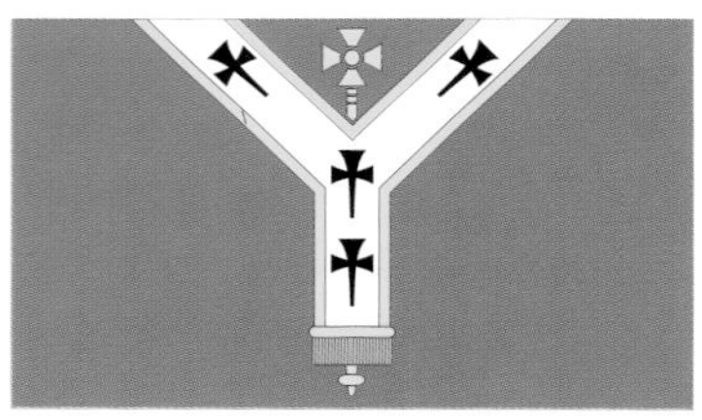

Archbishop of Canterbury
Primate of All England

Religious Organizations

Modern Britain has many religious faiths and some have flags. The Church of England has a flag for each diocese as well as armorial banners for bishops and cathedrals. Mosques and synagogues do not use flags, but mosques do have vexilloids (metal emblems on staffs) on their minarets and domes, and synagogues often show a *menora* or "Shield of David" emblem outside.

The Church of England
(with Diocesan Arms in the canton)

Westminster Abbey
(A Royal Peculiar)

Moderator of the General
Assembly of the Church of Scotland

Diocese of York

The Church in Wales

The Church of Scotland

Diocese of Brechin
Scottish Episcopal Church

The Salvation Army

Islamic Vexilloids

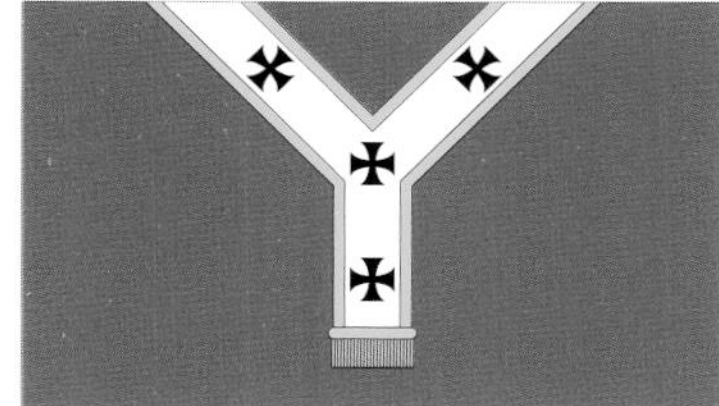

Cardinal Archbishop
of Westminster

The Buddhist Flag

Jewish Menora & Shield of David

The Holy See
Flown by Roman Catholic Churches

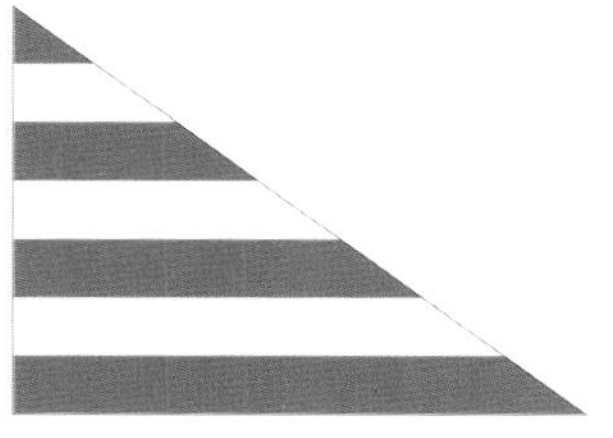

The *Dhvaja* of the Hindus

The *Khanda* Flag of the Sikhs

Boys' Brigade Queen's Colour

Youth Organizations

In addition to the military cadet organizations, covered in the armed forces section, Britain has many youth organizations that seek to promote self-development and self-confidence in young people. The oldest uniformed organization is the Boys' Brigade, founded by Sir William Smith in Glasgow in 1883. This was followed by the Girls' Brigade in 1893. In 1908 Lt-Gen Robert Baden-Powell started the Scout movement and in 1910 added the Girl Guides.

Boys' Brigade Company Ensign

Girls' Brigade Company Colour

Explorer Scout Unit Flag

Boys' Brigade St Andrew's Colour

World Scout Flag

Scout Troop Flag

Cub Pack Flag

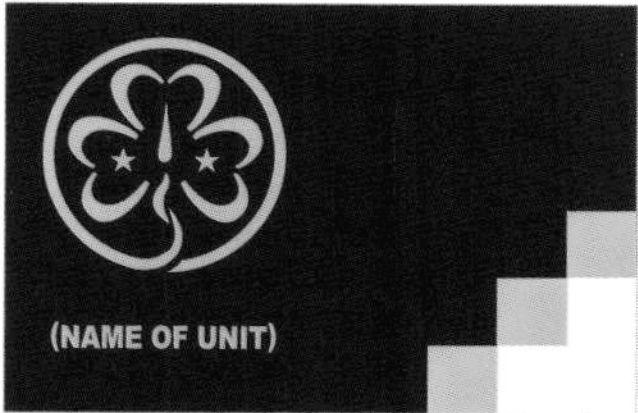

Girl Guide Company Flag

In addition to these flags some Sea Scout Units are warranted to wear a defaced Red Ensign with the Scout badge on their vessels. There is a matching burgee which should be flown along with the ensign.

Beaver Flag

Brownie Company Flag

Sea Scout Ensign

World Association of Girl Guides and Girl Scouts

Sea Scout Burgee

Queen's Award for Enterprise

Award Flags

The Queen's Awards Scheme was instituted by Royal Warrant in 1966 following the recommendations of a Committee chaired by HRH The Duke of Edinburgh. From 1975 until 1999 there were Queen's Awards for Export Achievement and Queen's Awards for Technological Achievement, with Queen's Awards for Environmental Achievement added in 1992. Since 2000 these have been combined in the Queen's Awards for Enterprise.

There are flags for all these awards that can be flown by companies or organizations that have won them. As the Awards last for five years the older designs are still current. The emblem on each flag can also be used on letterheads, signage and other material related to the company or organization..

To celebrate the 40th anniversary of the Queen's Accession, the Queen's Anniversary Prize was instituted in 1993 by the Queen's Anniversary Trust. It has been awarded on a biannual basis to academic institutions since 1994.

Queen's Award for Export Achievement

Queen's Award for Technological Achievement

Queen's Award for Environmental Achievement

Queen's Anniversary Prize

Heraldic Flags

In the Middle Ages a system of identifying knights, who were encased in armour during battles, was developed. It was named "Heraldry" after the Court Heralds who organized it, and recorded the different "coats of arms" that identified the knight. The system continues to this day and is governed by the College of Arms in England, Wales and Northern Ireland, and the Court of the Lord Lyon in Scotland. Today individuals and organizations can apply to the heraldic authorities for a grant of arms. Any coat of arms can be displayed as a banner, a rectangular flag which shows the same design as the shield of the arms. The Royal Standard is in fact such an armorial banner. The banner is the only heraldic flag commonly seen today.

The Banner of The Duke of Norfolk
Earl Marshal of England

Clan Flags and Badges

In Scotland heraldry is an integral part of the Clan system, with a variety of flags and emblems for each Clan. The badge of a clansman is his Chief's crest surrounded by a belt and buckle bearing the Clan's motto or slogan. This badge is usually made of silver or pewter and is worn on the hat or jacket. The Chief, Chieftains and other armigers (people with their own coat-of-arms) have slightly different badges. These show their own crest surrounded by a simple circlet bearing their motto. The circlet can be surmounted by a coronet of rank. In the case of a Chief there are three eagle feathers behind it, two for a Chieftain and one for an armiger (hence the saying "a feather in your cap").

Most clans also have one or more tartans, a woven cloth of symmetrical and repeating warp and weft. Designs can be registered with the Lord Lyon to protect them.

Badge of the
Chief of
Clan Graham

Badge of a
Graham
Clansman

The Standard of
The Duke of Montrose
Chief of Clan Graham
(*Ne Oublie* = Do Not Forget)

The Standard

The Chief has a standard to mark his "Headquarters", ie. he need not be there in person. The standard is a long tapering flag (usually from 120 centimetres down to 60 centimetres) with either the owner's arms or the National Flag at the hoist, with the tail in the main livery colours with the motto, usually on diagonal bands, separated by the owner's crest and other badges. The tail is split into two rounded ends (except those of Chiefs who are not peers or knights which have round unsplit ends) and the whole flag is fringed with alternating livery colours. The length varies in size depending upon the owner's rank:

The Sovereign	7.5 metres	Viscounts	5.0 metres
Dukes	6.5 metres	Barons	4.5 metres
Marquises	6.0 metres	Baronets	4.0 metres
Earls	5.5 metres	Knights & Feudal Barons	3.5 metres

The Banner of
The Duke of Montrose

The Banner

The Chief, Chieftains and other clan armigers all have personal banners that can only be used in the presence of the owner. They vary in size:

The Sovereign	1.50 metres square	Viscounts & Barons	1.00 metres square
Dukes	1.25 metres square	Baronets & Feudal Barons	0.90 metres square
Earls	1.10 metres square	Other Armigers	85 cm tall x 70 cm long

When flown from a house the standard it should be large enough to be intelligible at the height at which it is flown and have a width to length ratio of 4:5.

They also have smaller carrying flags which can be carried by the owner or his appointed henchman (the traditional title for clan officers).

The Pinsel

The delegated representative of a Chief has a flag called a pinsel. It is triangular, 0.60 metres high at the hoist and 1.35 metres long, with a background of the main livery colour of the Chief's arms. It shows the Chief's crest, within a strap and buckle bearing the motto, and outside the strap a gold or silver circlet inscribed with the Chief's or Baron's title. On top of this circlet is set the owner's coronet of rank or his baronial cap. In the fly is shown the owner's plant badge and a scroll inscribed with his slogan or motto. This flag is allotted only to Chiefs or very special Chieftain-barons for practical use by the Lord Lyon King of Arms.

The Guidon

Lairds who have a following, but are not peers or feudal barons have a flag called a guidon which is similar to a standard, but smaller. It is 2.40 metres long, tapering to a round unsplit end at the fly. It has a background of the livery colours, with the owner's crest or badge at the hoist and his motto in the fly.

The Pinsel of The Duke of Montrose
(*An Greumaich* = The Graham)

The Pinsel of The Macneil of Barra
Chief of Clan Macneil
(*Buaidh No Bas* = Victory or Death)

The Guidon of Macdonald of
Castle Camus, Lieutenant of Sleat

The Red Ensign
Britain's Civil Ensign

The Civil Jack

The Blue Ensign
Britain's Government Ensign

Flags at Sea

The main flags of a ship or boat are the Ensign, the Jack, the Burgee (for yachts) and sometimes a Courtesy Ensign. Royal Navy ships also have a masthead pennant.

The Ensign shows the Country of Registry of the vessel and is a requirement of international law (1956 Geneva Convention). Commissioned ships of the Royal Navy wear the White Ensign, ships in government service wear a defaced Blue Ensign, and most other civilian vessels wear the Red Ensign. Some organizations and many yacht clubs have been issued with Warrants permitting specific vessels owned by their members to wear either an undefaced Blue Ensign or a Blue or Red Ensign with a differentiating badge. Royal Research Ships, RN and RNR Captains and above, and certain others can wear the undefaced Blue Ensign. The Royal Yacht Squadron has a Warrant to wear the White Ensign. Wearing any flag other than an authorized Ensign is a breach of both British and international law.

The Jack is the flag that flies from the bow of a vessel, usually only in port. The Union Jack may only be used by ships of the Royal Navy. Government vessels fly square versions of their Blue Ensign. Civilian vessels fly the Civil Jack, or their House Flag if they belong to an organization. Vessels that took part in the Dunkirk evacuation have the special honour of flying the St. George's flag as their Jack.

The Burgee is a triangular flag that indicates the club to which the owner of the vessel belongs. The Burgee must match the Ensign that is being flown. Flag Officers of clubs replace their burgees with a Broad Pennant, which is "swallow-tailed" (ie. ends in two points). Past Flag Officers use rectangular versions of the Broad Pennant.

A Courtesy Ensign is a signal flag that acknowledges that the vessel is navigating in another country's territorial waters and that it will respect the laws and sovereignty of that country. It is normally a small replica of the country's civil ensign. Foreign vessels visiting the UK should hoist the White Ensign or Red Ensign as a courtesy ensign depending on whether they are warships or other vessels. It is an offence under the Merchant Shipping Act 1995 to fly the Union Flag as a courtesy ensign.

The Yacht Marina at the International Festival of the Sea in Portsmouth, August 2001

The Position of the Flags

The senior position on a vessel is as near to the stern as possible and is reserved for the ensign. In practice in most modern sailing yachts this is at the taffrail. A ketch or yawl, finding this impossible whilst sailing, perhaps because of the boom, should choose the next nearest position. The head of the mizzen mast is usually preferable to the peak or leech of the mizzen sail due to the difficulty of saluting. When sailing finishes the ensign should be returned to its rightful place.

The next senior position is the main masthead. It is reserved for the burgee or house flag. More than one flag may be flown on a single halyard. No flag can be above the burgee on the same halyard, nor any flag above the courtesy ensign on its halyard. The burgee must always be higher than the ensign.

The starboard spreaders are for signalling and the port spreaders are for House Flags etc. Courtesy ensigns, as signals, should be flown from the starboard spreaders.

When to Wear Ensigns

Ensigns should be worn, whilst at sea, whenever another vessel is in sight or within the territorial waters of another country (unless racing). When at anchor or in harbour they should be worn as follows: between November 1st and February 14th, from 9am (local time) to Sunset; for the rest of the year from 8am to 9pm. Sunrise and Sunset always override these times. The lowering of the flags ("Striking Colours") is traditionally a time to remember all those who gave their lives in the service of the flag.

The timing is taken as follows: firstly from a vessel of The Royal Navy; failing that from a Naval Shore Establishment; failing that from the senior Royal Yacht Club at the port; failing that from the Senior Flag Officer present; failing all of the above from the ship's clock.

The only flags not lowered at 9pm/Sunset are the Commissioning Pennant of a warship and the Broad Pennants of Yacht Club Flag Officers. These remain flying 24 hours a day.

HMS *Warrior* dressed overall, complete with the Ensigns and Pennant of the pre-1865 Red Squadron

Dressing Ship

There are two ways of dressing ship: with Masthead Flags when under way (or by small vessels without dressing lines) or over all (Rainbow Fashion) only when not under way.

Flags flown when dressing with Masthead Flags are the ensign, plus ensigns of the same size repeated at each mast head, plus the burgee alongside the ensign at the mainmast. For foreign festivals one masthead ensign is replaced by the relevant courtesy ensign (the mainmast on single-masted vessels, the second mast if more than one).

Vessels dressed overall will fly the flags as above adding dressing lines (ie. a single halyard with many signal flags on it). The recommended order is from bow to stern: E, Q, numeral pennant 3, G, numeral pennant 8, Z, numeral pennant 4, W, numeral pennant 6, P, numeral pennant 1, I, Code, T, Y, B, X, 1st substitute, H, 3rd substitute, D, F, 2nd substitute, U, A, O, M, K, numeral pennant 2, J, numeral pennant 0, N, numeral pennant 9, K, numeral pennant 7, V, numeral pennant 5, L, C, S. As a guide, in a single-masted vessel the divide at the masthead would be between the 3rd substitute and D, and in a twin-masted vessel Y to numeral pennant 0 would be between the masts. These positions vary from vessel to vessel and flag manufacturers will offer guidance as to the best separation for a particular vessel, based on its overall length, mast heights and positions. For warships, the order of flags and pennants is laid down for each class of ship.

Mourning and Half-masting

For National Mourning the ensign and any jack are half-masted until the next time for striking Colours. For Private Mourning within a club, the club burgee is half-masted as well. A flag is always hoisted "close up" (fully up) on raising and lowering before and after being placed at half-mast. Other than on the death of the Sovereign, flags are not half-masted again until the day of the funeral when they are raised immediately after the interment.

Saluting

Saluting ("doffing your cap") is carried out by "dipping" the ensign to a position $^1/_3$ of the way up the ensign staff. There it remains until the saluted vessel dips in acknowledgement (or passes out of sight). Civilian vessels should salute any warship (only the senior ship in a convoy) and vessels carrying a member of the Royal Family or head of state (or their representative). Yachts should also salute flag officers of the owner's club.

Royal National Lifeboat Institution (RNLI) Jack & House Flag

Maritime Organizations

There are flags for the sea rescue service (the RNLI) and for the three lighthouse authorities (Trinity House, Northern Lights and Irish Lights). These include ensigns, house flags, officers' flags and members' flags. The maritime underwriters Lloyd's of London, the Marine Society, the Maritime Volunteer Service and the Company of Watermen and Lightermen all have their own ensigns.

RNLI Ensign

Trinity House Jack & House Flag

Deputy Master of Trinity House

RNLI Member
(also used in burgee form)

Master of Trinity House
(HRH The Duke of Edinburgh)

Trinity House Ensign

Northern Lights Ensign

Irish Lights Ensign

Marine Society Ensign

Northern Lights Commissioners' Flag (uses pre-1801 Union Flag)

Irish Lights Commissioners' Flag

Maritime Volunteer Service Ensign

Northern Lights Commissioners' Pennant

Lloyd's of London Ensign

Company of Watermen and Lightermen Ensign

Three of Britain's Port and Harbour Authorities have their own defaced Blue Ensigns, and three of the Sea Fisheries organizations have their own defaced Red Ensigns. The rest use undefaced Red Ensigns. Some cable ships belonging to Global Marine Systems fly the old Post Office Ensign.

Port of London Authority House Flag

Port of London Authority Ensign

Aberdeen Harbour Board Ensign

Port of London Authority Chairman

Eastern Sea Fisheries Ensign

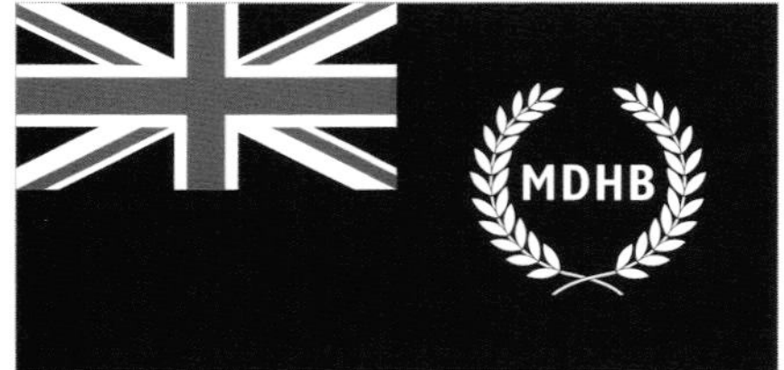

Mersey Docks and Harbour Company Ensign

Port of London Authority Vice Chairman

North Wales and North West Sea Fisheries Ensign

South Wales Sea Fisheries Ensign

Shipping is still important to Britain as an island nation. Some of the world's great shipping lines are British. Each line has a company flag that usually flies in place of the civil jack in port and from the masthead when underway.

Cunard

Global Marine Systems Cable Ships Ensign

BP Shipping

Peninsular & Oriental (P&O)

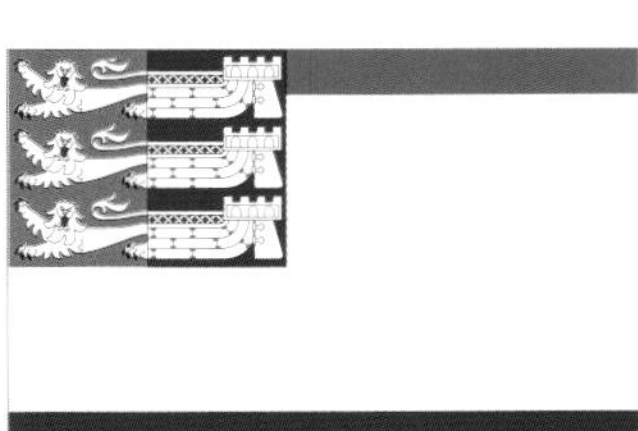

Port of Dover House Flag

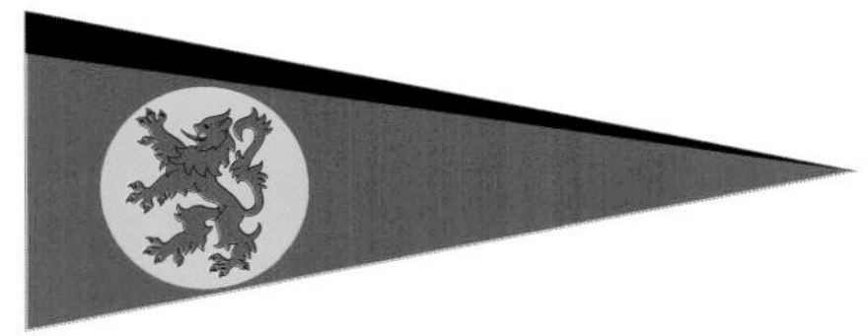

Caledonian-MacBrayne

Shell

Yacht Club Ensigns and Burgees

The following United Kingdom Yacht Clubs are authorized by the Ministry of Defence to wear ensigns other than the plain Red Ensign. The yacht must wear the matching Burgee.

Undefaced White Ensign

The Royal Yacht Squadron, alone, is privileged to wear the White Ensign.

The White Ensign

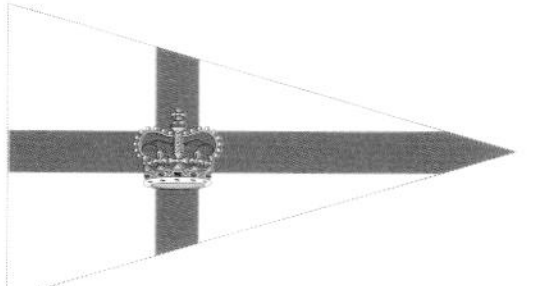

Royal Yacht Squadron Burgee

Undefaced Blue Ensigns

The following Yacht Clubs are privileged to wear an undefaced Blue Ensign. Only the Burgees are shown:

The Blue Ensign

Royal Albert Yacht Club Burgee

Royal Cinque Ports Yacht Club Burgee

Royal Cruising Club Burgee

Royal Dorset Yacht Club Burgee

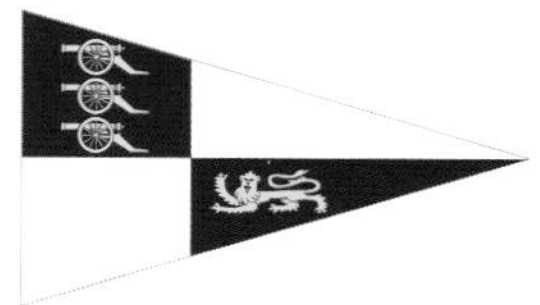

Royal Engineer Yacht Club Burgee

Royal Gourock Yacht Club Burgee

Royal Highland Yacht Club Burgee

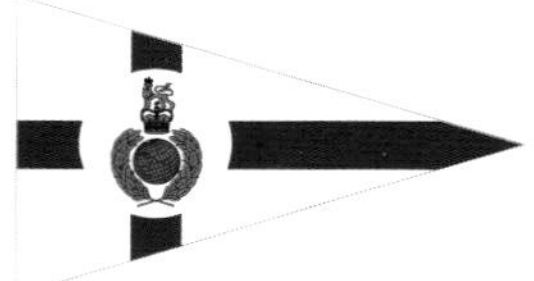

Royal Marines Sailing Club Burgee

Royal Motor Yacht Club Burgee

Royal Naval Sailing Association Burgee

Royal Solent Yacht Club Burgee

Royal Western Yacht Club (England) Burgee

Royal Naval Volunteer Reserve Yacht Club Burgee

Royal Southern Yacht Club Burgee

Royal Western Yacht Club (Scotland) Burgee

Royal Northern and Clyde Yacht Club Burgee

Royal Temple Yacht Club Burgee

Sussex Motor Yacht Club Burgee

Royal Scottish Motor Yacht Club Burgee

Royal Thames Yacht Club Burgee

Defaced Blue Ensigns

The following Yacht Clubs are privileged to wear Blue Ensigns defaced with a badge. For each Club both the Ensign and the Burgee are shown:

Army Sailing Association Ensign

City Livery Yacht Club Ensign

The Cruising Association Ensign

Army Sailing Association Burgee

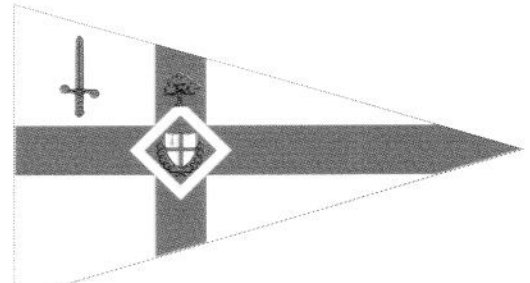
City Livery Yacht Club Burgee

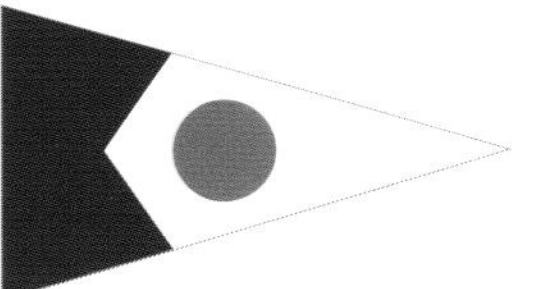
The Cruising Association Burgee

Aldeburgh Yacht Club Ensign

Bar Yacht Club Ensign

Conway Club Cruising Association Ensign

The House of Lords Yacht Club Ensign

Aldeburgh Yacht Club Burgee

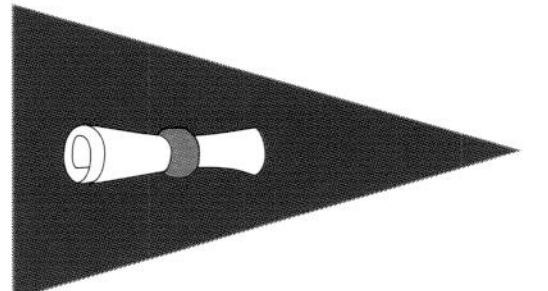
Bar Yacht Club Burgee

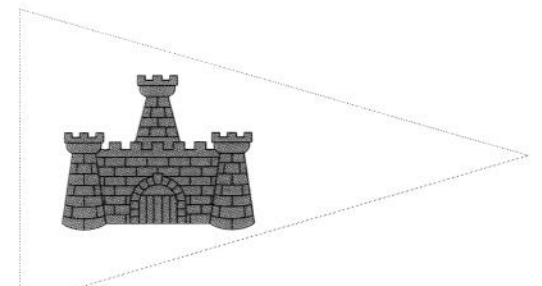
Conway Club Cruising Association Burgee

The House of Lords Yacht Club Burgee

Household Division Yacht Club Ensign

Medway Cruising Club Ensign

Old Worcesters Yacht Club Ensign

Poole Harbour Yacht Club Ensign

Household Division Yacht Club Burgee

Medway Cruising Club Burgee

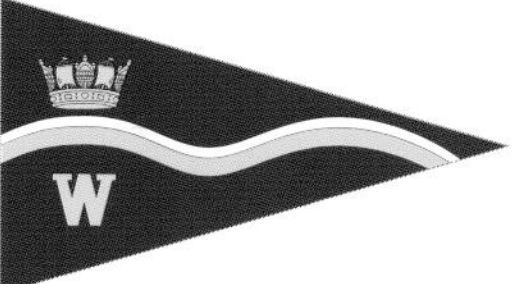

Old Worcesters Yacht Club Burgee

Poole Harbour Yacht Club Burgee

Little Ship Club Ensign

The Medway Yacht Club Ensign

Parkstone Yacht Club Ensign

Poole Yacht Club Ensign

Little Ship Club Burgee

The Medway Yacht Club Burgee

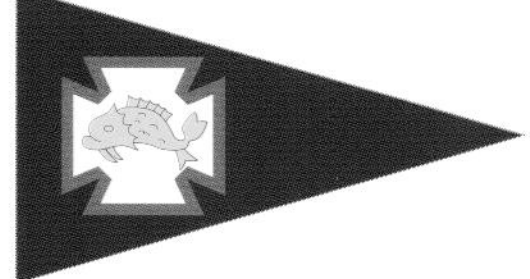

Parkstone Yacht Club Burgee

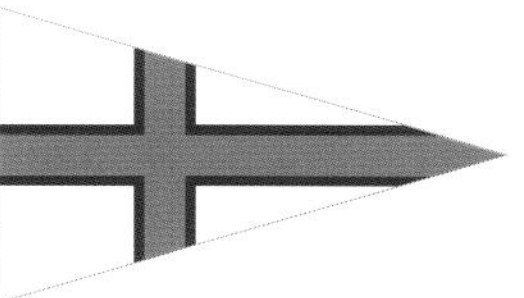

Poole Yacht Club Burgee

Royal Air Force Yacht Club Ensign

Royal Armoured Corps Yacht Club Ensign

Royal Bermuda Yacht Club Ensign

Royal Channel Islands Yacht Club Ensign

Royal Air Force Yacht Club Burgee

Royal Armoured Corps Yacht Club Burgee

Royal Bermuda Yacht Club Burgee

Royal Channel Islands Yacht Club Burgee

Royal Anglesey Yacht Club Ensign

Royal Artillery Yacht Club Ensign

Royal Burnham Yacht Club Ensign

Royal Corinthian Yacht Club Ensign

Royal Anglesey Yacht Club Burgee

Royal Artillery Yacht Club Burgee

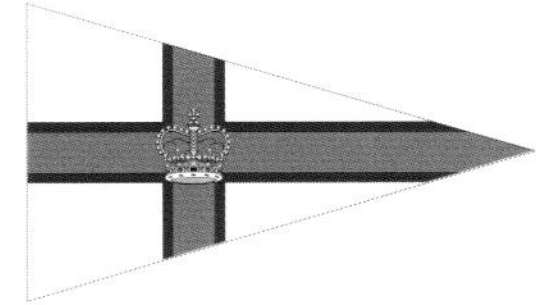

Royal Burnham Yacht Club Burgee

Royal Corinthian Yacht Club Burgee

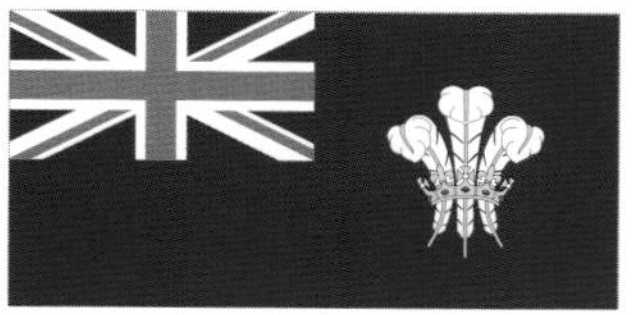
Royal Cornwall Yacht Club Ensign

Royal Forth Yacht Club Ensign

Royal Harwich Yacht Club Ensign

Royal Mersey Yacht Club Ensign

Royal Cornwall Yacht Club Burgee

Royal Forth Yacht Club Burgee

Royal Harwich Yacht Club Burgee

Royal Mersey Yacht Club Burgee

Royal Dee Yacht Club Ensign

Royal Gibraltar Yacht Club Ensign

Royal London Yacht Club Ensign

Royal North of Ireland Yacht Club Ensign

Royal Dee Yacht Club Burgee

Royal Gibraltar Yacht Club Burgee

Royal London Yacht Club Burgee

Royal North of Ireland Yacht Club Burgee

Royal Northumberland Yacht Club Ensign

Royal Plymouth Corinthian Yacht Club Ensign

Royal Torbay Yacht Club Ensign

Royal Welsh Yacht Club Ensign

Royal Northumberland Yacht Club Burgee

Royal Plymouth Corinthian Yacht Club Burgee

Royal Torbay Yacht Club Burgee

Royal Welsh Yacht Club Burgee

Royal Ocean Racing Club Ensign

Royal Southampton Yacht Club Ensign

Royal Ulster Yacht Club Ensign

Royal Yorkshire Yacht Club Ensign

Royal Ocean Racing Club Burgee

Royal Southampton Yacht Club Burgee

Royal Ulster Yacht Club Burgee

Royal Yorkshire Yacht Club Burgee

Severn Motor Yacht Club
Ensign

Severn Motor Yacht Club
Burgee

Sussex Yacht Club
Ensign

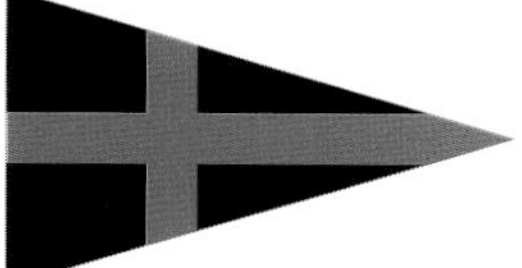

Sussex Yacht Club
Burgee

Thames Motor Yacht Club
Ensign

Thames Motor Yacht Club
Burgee

Defaced Red Ensigns

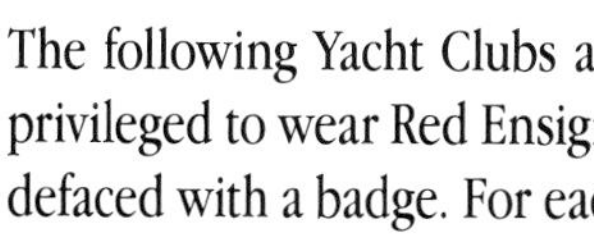

The following Yacht Clubs are privileged to wear Red Ensigns defaced with a badge. For each Club both the Ensign and the Burgee are shown:

Brixham Yacht Club
Ensign

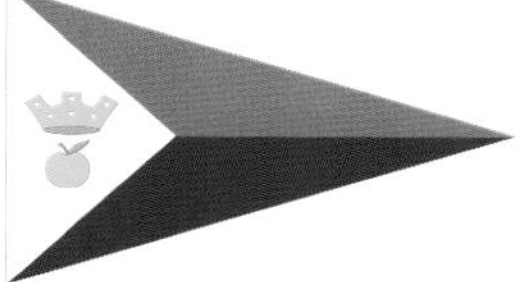

Brixham Yacht Club
Burgee

House of Commons
Yacht Club Ensign

House of Commons
Yacht Club Burgee

Lloyd's Yacht Club
Ensign

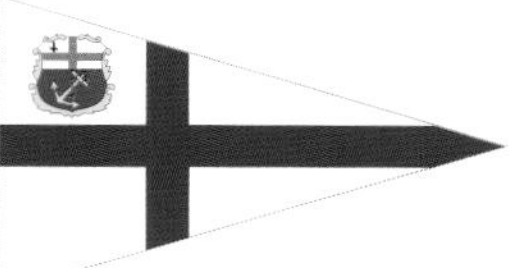

Lloyd's Yacht Club
Burgee

Royal Dart Yacht Club Ensign

Royal Hamilton Amateur Dinghy Club Ensign

Royal Norfolk and Suffolk Yacht Club Ensign

Royal Windermere Yacht Club Ensign

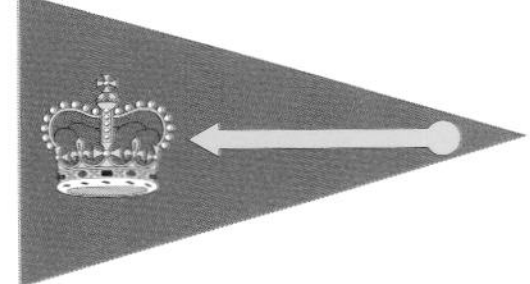

Royal Dart Yacht Club Burgee

Royal Hamilton Amateur Dinghy Club Burgee

Royal Norfolk and Suffolk Yacht Club Burgee

Royal Windermere Yacht Club Burgee

Royal Fowey Yacht Club Ensign

Royal Lymington Yacht Club Ensign

Royal Victoria Yacht Club Ensign

St. Helier Yacht Club Ensign

Royal Fowey Yacht Club Burgee

Royal Lymington Yacht Club Burgee

Royal Victoria Yacht Club Burgee

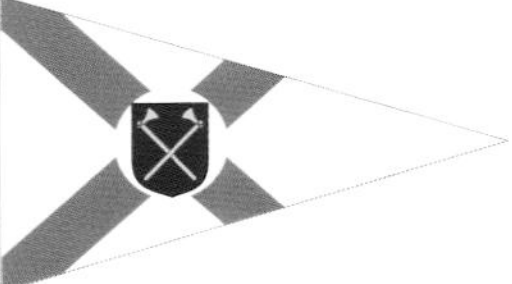

St. Helier Yacht Club Burgee

West Mersea Yacht Club Ensign

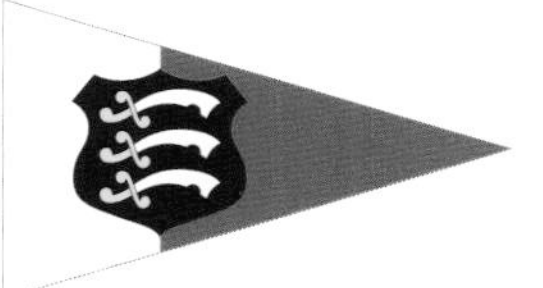
West Mersea Yacht Club Burgee

Royal Yachting Association Official Duty Ensign

Royal Yachting Association Official Duty Burgee

The Royal Yachting Association (RYA) Ensign and Burgee can only be used by RYA officers on official duty. Other members can fly the hoist flag below (or the burgee form):

RYA Member (also used in burgee form)

Defaced RAF Ensign

The RAF Sailing Association is privileged to wear an RAF Ensign defaced with the RAF badge:

RAF Sailing Association Ensign

RAF Sailing Association Burgee

Signal Flags

Modern signalling with flags uses the International Code of Signals:

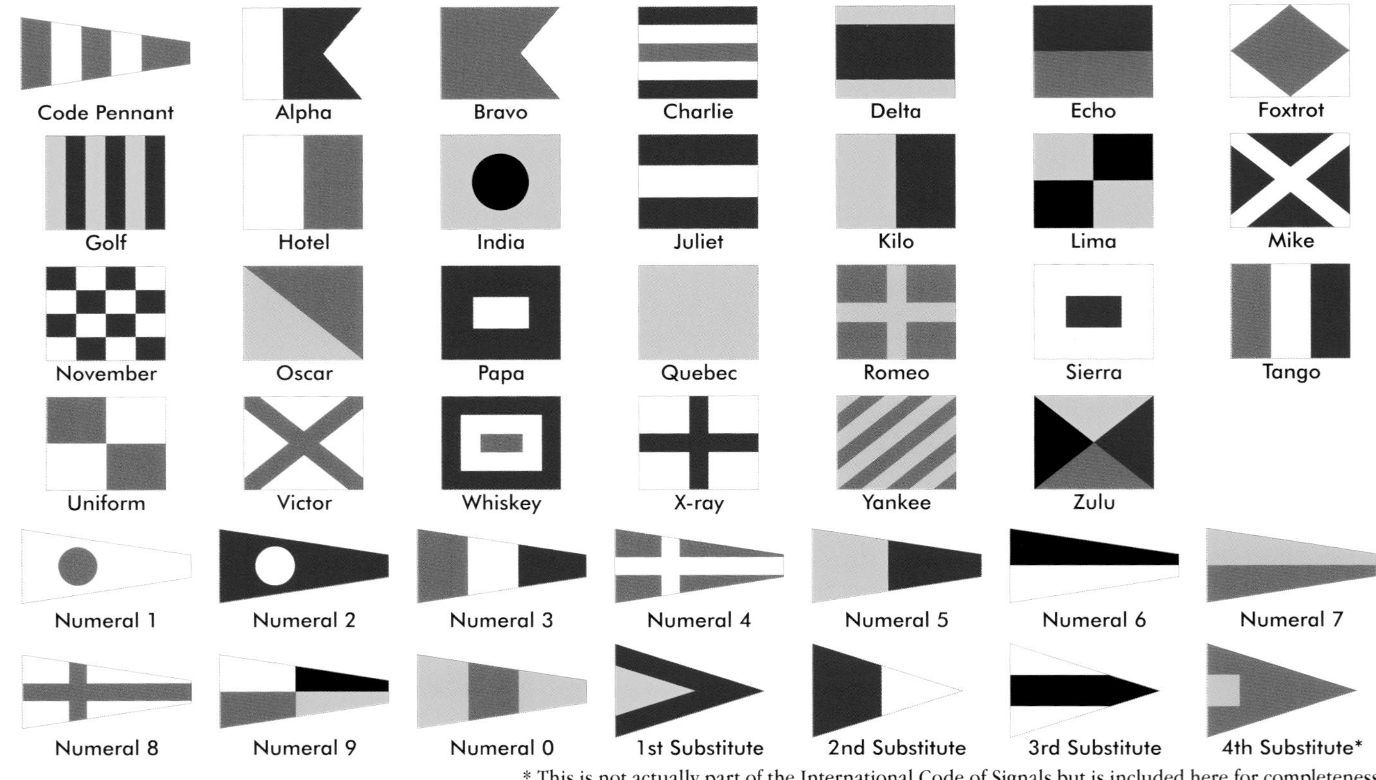

* This is not actually part of the International Code of Signals but is included here for completeness

Although the code consists of flags representing letters, it is not an alphabetic code. Each letter, if flown on its own, has a specific meaning. For more complex messages the flags are combined into sets of up to five flags; the combination is then looked up in a code book to obtain the meaning.

The single flag meanings are:

Alpha	I have a diver down; keep clear at slow speed
Bravo	I am taking in, or discharging, or carrying dangerous goods
Charlie	Yes (affirmative)
Delta	Keep clear of me; I am manoeuvring with difficulty
Echo	I am altering my course to starboard
Foxtrot	I am disabled; communicate with me
Golf	I require a pilot. When made by fishing vessels on or near fishing grounds it means "I am hauling nets"
Hotel	I have a pilot on board
India	I am altering my course to port
Juliet	Keep well clear of me. I am on fire and have dangerous cargo on board, or I am leaking dangerous cargo
Kilo	I wish to communicate with you
Lima	You should stop your vessel instantly
Mike	My vessel is stopped and making no way through the water
November	No (negative)
Oscar	Man overboard
Papa	The Blue Peter - all aboard, vessel is about to proceed to sea (in harbour); my nets have come fast upon an obstruction (fishing vessels at sea)
Quebec	My vessel is healthy and I request free pratique
Romeo	*No meaning*
Sierra	I am operating astern propulsion
Tango	Keep clear of me; I am engaged in pair trawling
Uniform	You are running into danger
Victor	I require assistance
Whiskey	I require medical assistance
X-ray	Stop carrying out your intentions and watch for my signals
Yankee	I am dragging my anchor
Zulu	I require a tug. When made by fishing vessels on or near fishing grounds it means "I am shooting nets"

HMS *Montrose* shows her identity "GCOD" in a signal hoist

Some of the two flag signals (topmost flag first) are:

AC I am abandoning my vessel
AE I must abandon my vessel
AF I do not intend to abandon my vessel
AN I need a doctor
AQ I have injured/sick person to be taken off urgently
BR I require a helicopter
CB I require immediate assistance
CB4 ditto - I am aground
CB5 ditto - I am drifting
CB6 ditto - I am on fire
CB7 ditto - I have sprung a leak
CK Assistance is not (or is no longer) required by me (or vessel indicated)
CV I am unable to give assistance
CP I am proceeding to your assistance
DV I am drifting
DX I am sinking (lat...long...if necessary)
ED Your distress signals are understood
EF SOS/MAYDAY has been cancelled
EL Repeat the distress position
FA Will you give me my position?
FO I will keep close to you
GW Man overboard; please take action to pick him up
IL I can only proceed at slow speed
IT I am on fire
IZ Fire has been extinguished
JG I am aground; I am in dangerous situation
JH I am aground; I am not in danger
JI Are you aground?
JL You are running the risk of going aground
JW I have sprung a leak
JX Leak is gaining rapidly
KJ I am towing a submerged object
KM I can take you in tow
KN I cannot take you in tow
KQ Prepare to be taken in tow
KR All is ready for towing
KT1 I am sending a towing hawser
LBI Towing hawser is fast to chain cable
LG You should prepare to cast off hawser
LO I am not in my correct position: used by a light vessel
NC I am in distress and require immediate assistance
NF You are running into danger
NG You are in a dangerous position
NH You are clear of all dangers
OQ I am calibrating radio direction finder or adjusting compasses
PD Your navigation lights are not visible
PH You should steer as indicated
PI You should maintain your present course
PN You should keep to leeward of me (or vessel indicated)
PP Keep well clear of me
QO You should not come alongside
QP I will come alongside
QR I cannot come alongside
QT You should not anchor. You are going to foul my anchor
QU Anchoring is prohibited
QX I request permission to anchor
RA My anchor is foul
RB I am dragging my anchor
RN My engines are out of action
RU Keep clear of me; I am manoeuvring with difficulty
SO You should stop your vessel instantly
TP Fishing gear has fouled my propeller
UM The harbour is closed to traffic
UN You may enter harbour immediately
UO You must not enter harbour
UP Permission to enter harbour is urgently requested. I have an emergency
UW I wish you a pleasant voyage
UY I am carrying out exercises - keep clear of me
YG You appear not to be complying with the traffic separation scheme
YU I am going to communicate with your station by means of the International Code of Signals
ZD2 Please report me to Lloyd's, London
ZL Your signal has been received but not understood
ZM You should send (or speak) more slowly

Additional Naval Signal Flags

To carry out visual signalling the Royal Navy (and the other NATO navies) use an extra set of flags. These include an additional set of numeral flags which are used for signalling plain numbers (as opposed to numerical codes), flags to indicate who the message is for, pennants to signal speed, course changes, and a special pennant which is flown when a ship is holding an act of worship, the church pennant.

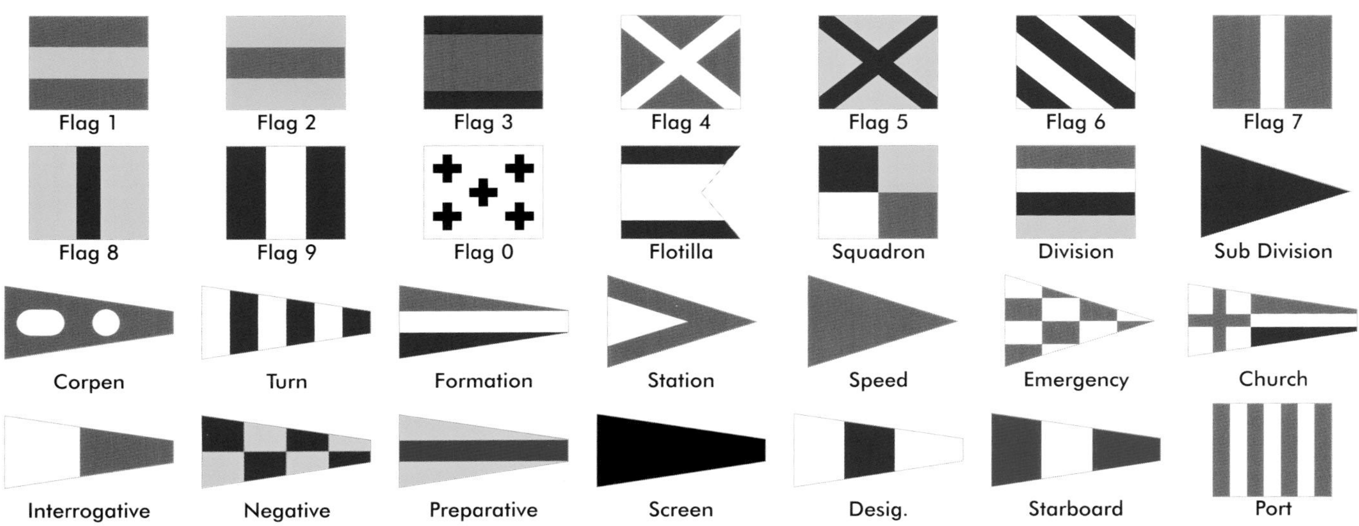

Royal and Noble Rank Insignia

The main mark of rank within Royalty and the Nobility is by the coronet, which has different emblems around the top edge of the rim. The Robes of Estate or Coronation Robes (on the left) differ by the number of ermine tails (black spots) on the cape, while the Parliamentary Robes (on the right) differ by the number of fur bands down the side.

Heir Apparent

Sovereign's Child†

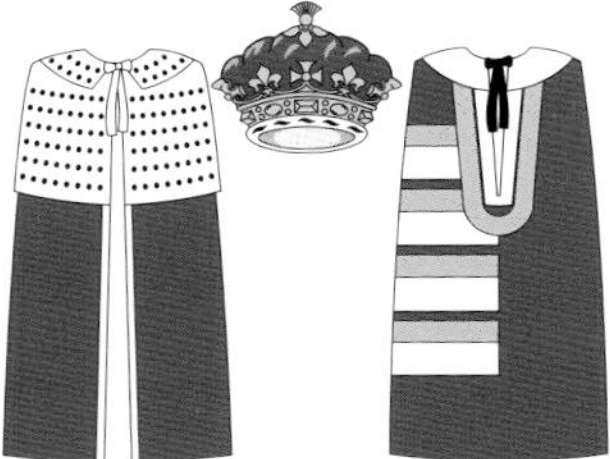
Sovereign's Grandchild†
(in the direct line)

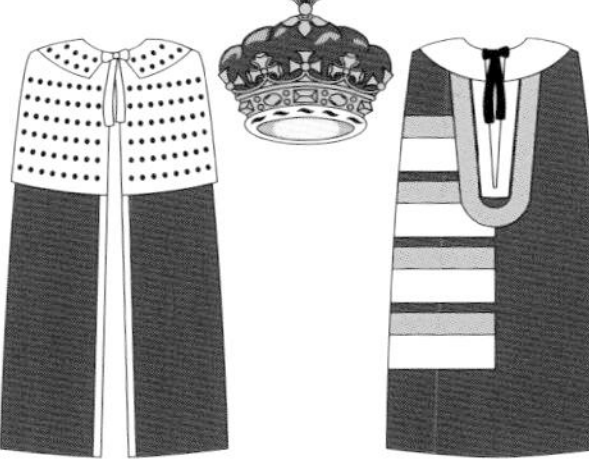
Sovereign's Grandchild†
(child of a younger son)

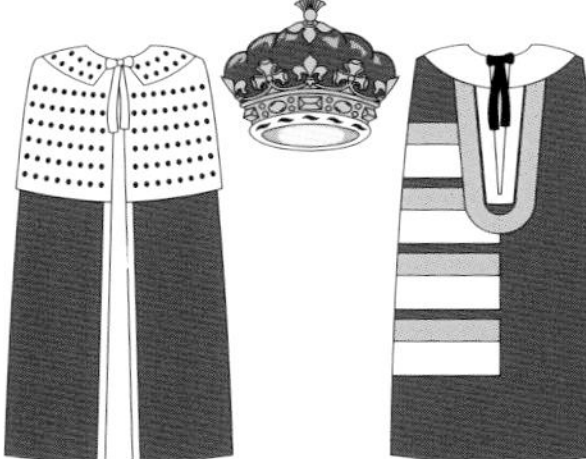
Sovereign's Grandchild†
(child of a daughter)

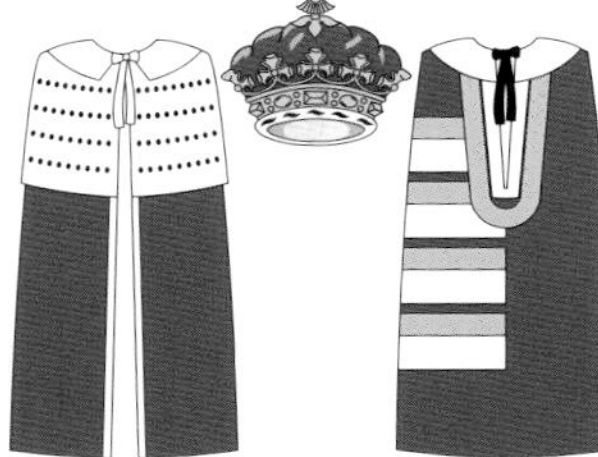
Duke

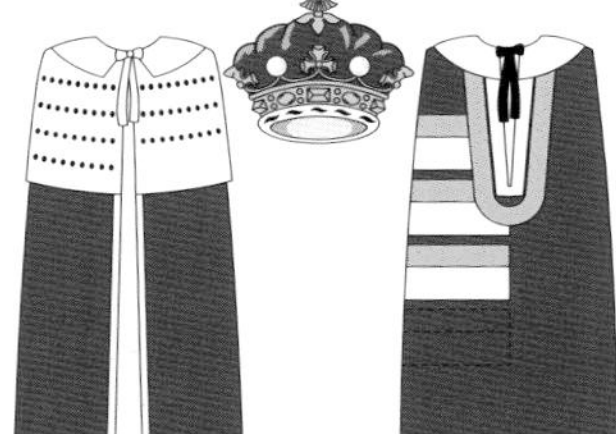
Marquis*

Earl

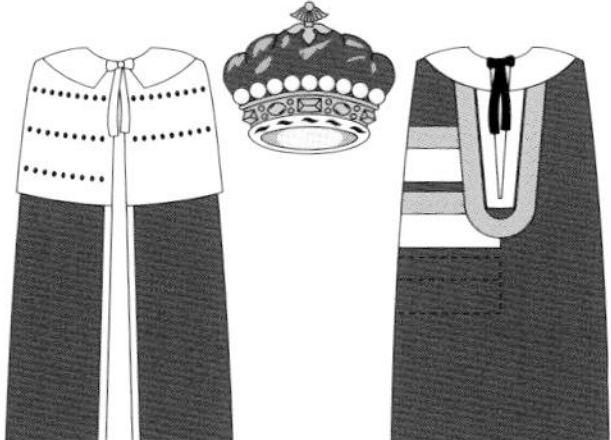
Viscount*

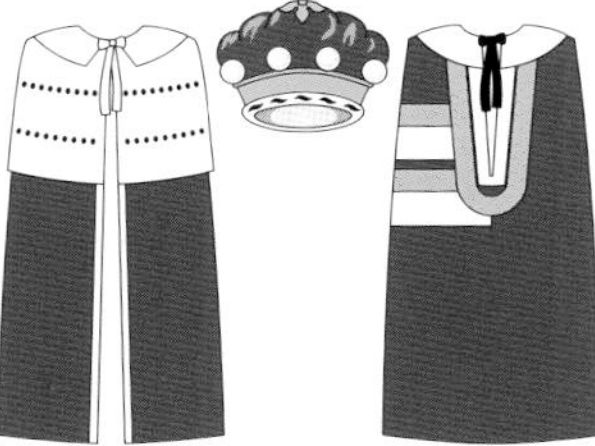
Baron

† The actual robes worn depend upon the person's title. Those of a Royal Duke are shown. * Dotted lines indicate a band only on the back of the robe.

Royal Navy Rank Insignia

Royal Navy officer ranks are shown by shoulder boards and gold rings on the jacket cuffs. RNR officers have a small 'R' in the centre of the ring.

Admiral of the Fleet

Admiral

Vice Admiral

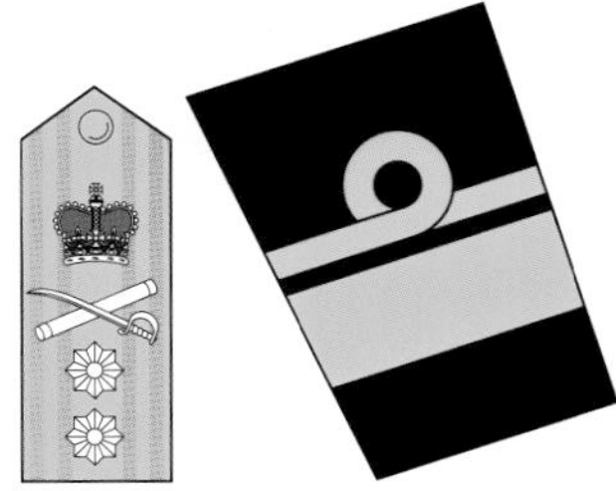

Rear Admiral

Commodore

Captain

Commander

Lieutenant Commander

Lieutenant
(red fill for medical)

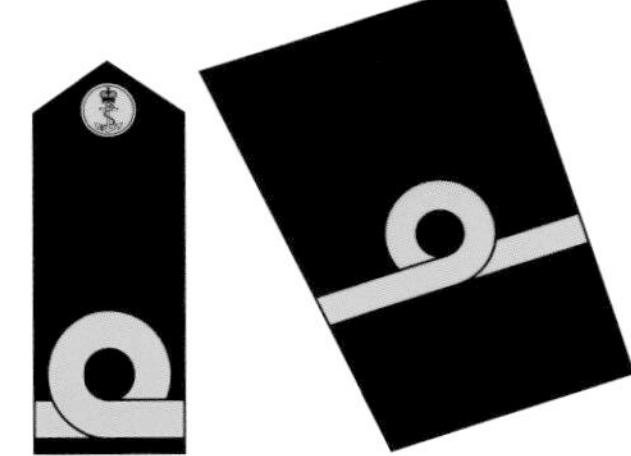

Sub Lieutenant

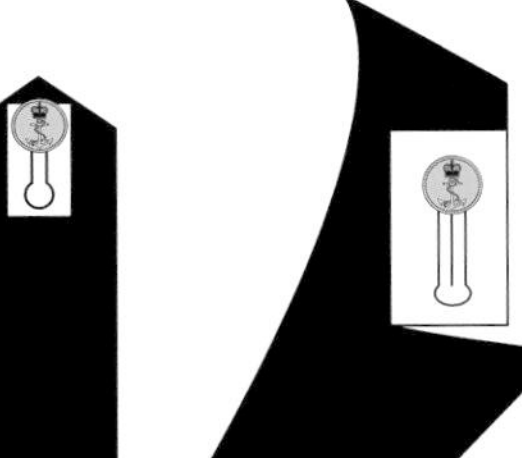

Midshipman

Royal Marines Rank Insignia

RM officer ranks are indicated by shoulder boards and use the same emblems as the Army, with the addition of "RM" to ranks below Colonel.

Field Marshal†

General

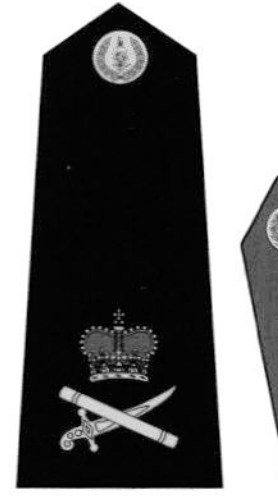

Lieutenant General

Major General

Brigadier

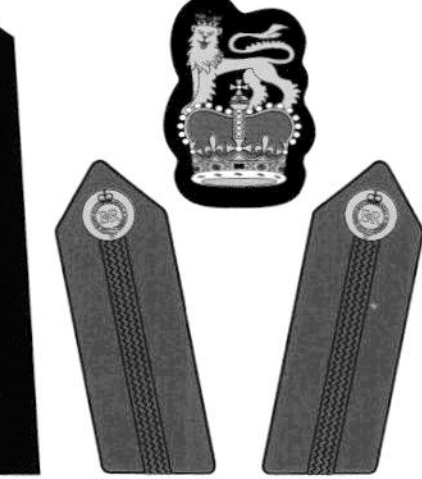

Colonel

Lieutenant Colonel

Major

Captain

Lieutenant

Second Lieutenant

† This is not a normal Royal Marines rank, but their Captain-General, HRH The Duke of Edinburgh, is a Field Marshal and wears these insignia when in Royal Marine uniform.

British Army Rank Insignia

Army officer ranks are shown by shoulder straps and senior officers have gorget patches on their jacket collars and wear special cap badges.

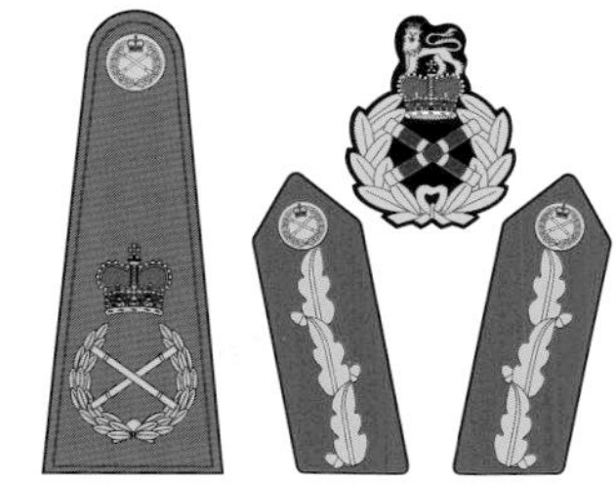
Field Marshal

General

Lieutenant General

Major General

Brigadier

Colonel

Lieutenant Colonel

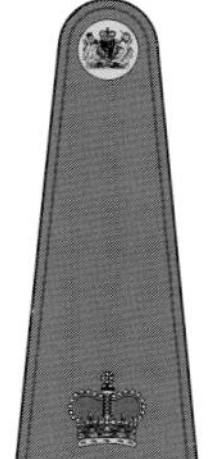
Major

Captain

Lieutenant

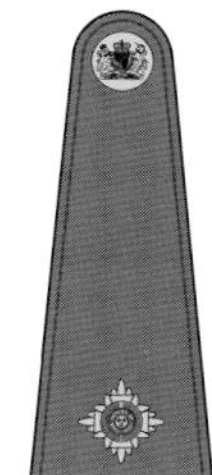
Second Lieutenant

Royal Air Force Rank Insignia

RAF officer ranks are shown by lace rings on the jacket cuffs or on sholder straps. The rank titles are a mixture of naval and military styles.

Marshal of the RAF

Air Chief Marshal

Air Marshal

Air Vice-Marshal

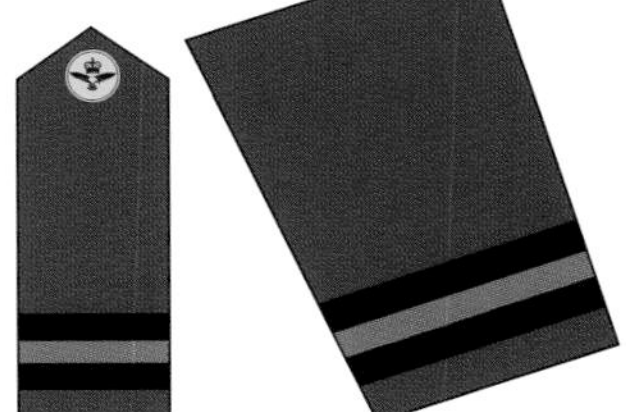
Air Commodore

Group Captain

Wing Commander

Squadron Leader

Flight Lieutenant

Flying Officer

Pilot Officer

NCO and Warrant Officer Rank Insignia

Non-commissioned officers (NCOs) and Warrant Officers usually wear their insignia as embroidered patches on their sleeves. Only the basic ranks and insignia are shown here.

Royal Navy

Warrant Officer

Chief Petty Officer (3 sleeve buttons)

Petty Officer

Leading Rate

British Army

Warrant Officer Class 1

Warrant Officer Class 2a (top) & 2b

Staff Sergeant

Sergeant

Corporal/ Bombardier

Lance Corporal/ Lance Bombardier

Royal Air Force

Warrant Officer

Flight Sergeant

Chief Technician

Sergeant

Corporal

Junior Technician

HM Coastguard Rank Insignia

Coastguard ranks are shown by Navy-style gold rings on their jacket cuffs and shoulder strap slip-ons.

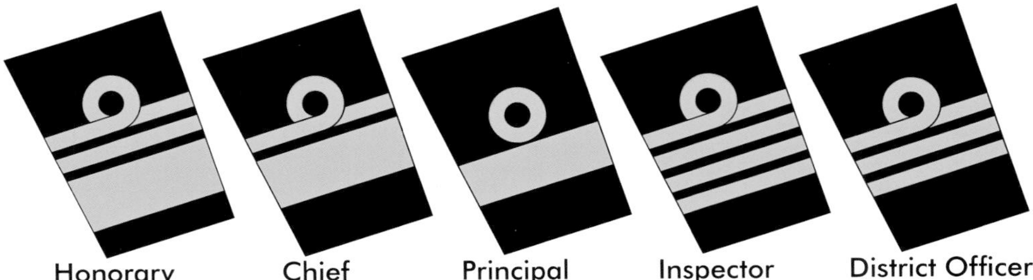

Honorary Commodore | Chief Coastguard | Principal Officer | Inspector (Area Ops Mgr) | District Officer (District Ops Mgr)

Asst Dist Officer DDC Ops Mgr | ADO Watch/Sector Mgr | Watch Officer | Coastguard Watch Assistant

H.M. COASTGUARD

Station Officer

H.M. COASTGUARD

Deputy Station Officer

Auxiliary Coastguard

HM Customs & Excise Rank Insignia

Customs officers also use Navy-style gold rings on their jacket cuffs. Senior officers do not wear uniforms.

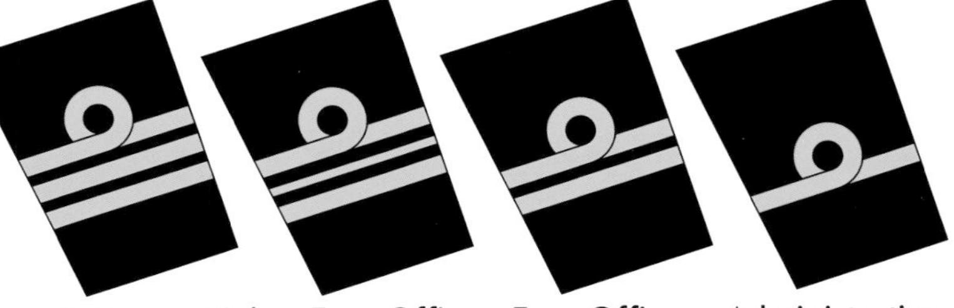

Cutter Commander | Higher Exec Officer (Band 7/8) | Exec Officer (Band 5/6) | Administrative Officer (Band 4)

H.M. CUSTOMS AND EXCISE

Revenue Constable

Merchant Navy Rank Insignia

Merchant Navy officer ranks are shown by shoulder boards and gold rings on the jacket cuffs. They differ in style from those of the Royal Navy, using diamonds rather than curls. Engineering officers have purple backgrounds to their rings, electrical engineers have green, medical officers have red and pursers have white. The ring designs vary between the various shipping companies.

Captain / Master

Chief Officer / Chief Mate

2nd Officer / 2nd Mate

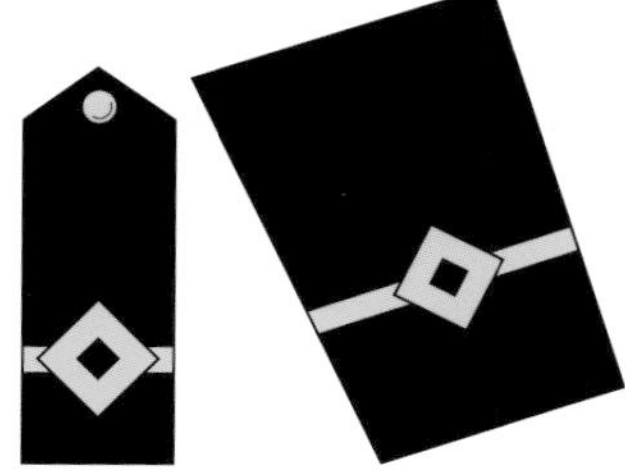

3rd Officer / 3rd Mate

Chief Engineering Officer

2nd Engineer

Electrical Engineer (green edges)

Medical Officer (red edges)

Purser (white edges)

Cadet

Police Service Rank Insignia

Police ranks are shown by shoulder boards and closely follow the Army's insignia. Senior officers have crossed tip-staffs, the ancient symbol of a law officer, within a laurel garland. The Metropolitan and City of London Police have a slightly different rank structure from the other police services, having a Commissioner rather than a Chief Constable.

Commissioner

Deputy Commissioner

Assistant Commissioner or Chief Constable

Deputy Asst. Commissioner or Deputy Chief Constable

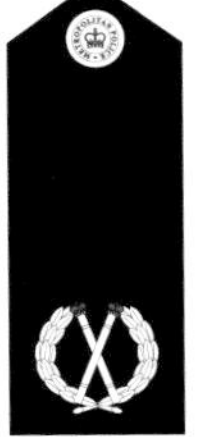

Commander or Assistant Chief Constable

Chief Superintendent

Superintendent

Chief Inspector

Inspector

Sergeant

Fire Service Rank Insignia

Operationally, Fire Service ranks are shown by the helmet colour and black stripe markings. The undress and fire uniforms have shoulder straps marked with impellers.

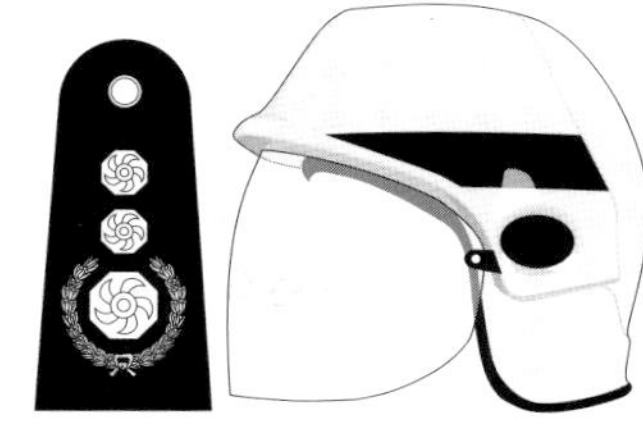
Chief Officer

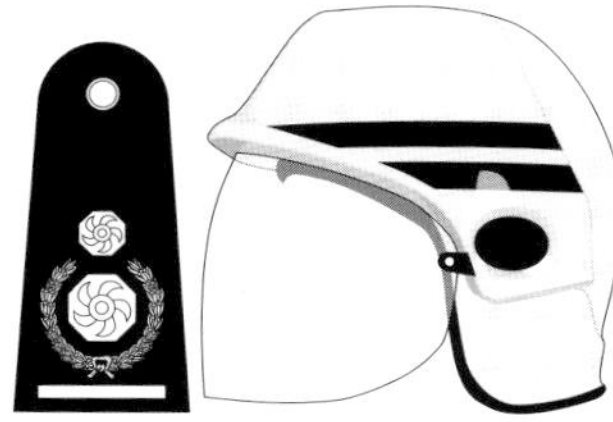
Deputy Chief Officer

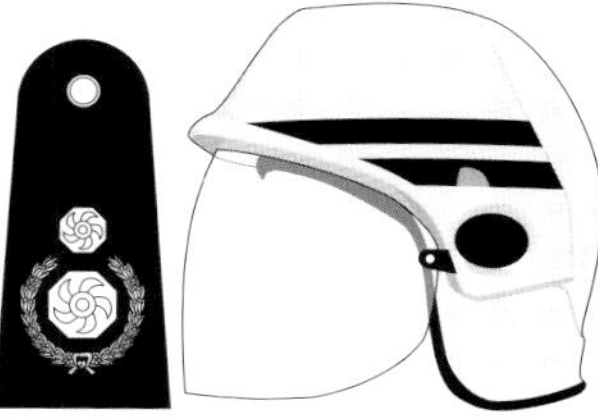
Chief Staff Officer / Assistant Chief Officer

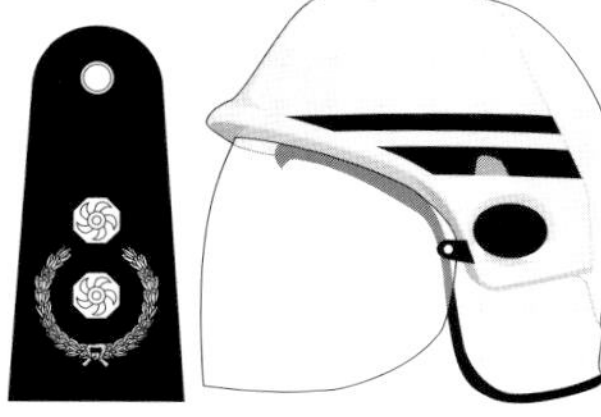
Deputy Assistant Chief Officer

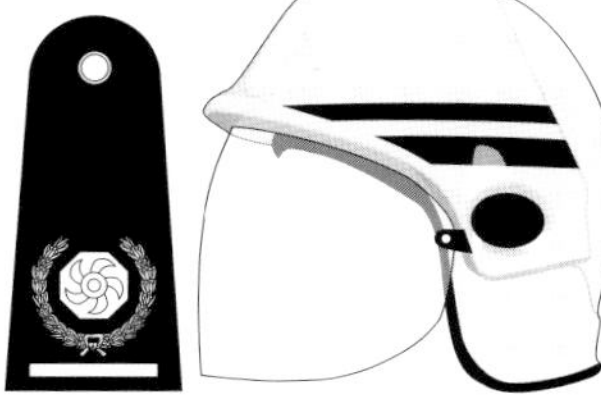
Senior Divisional Officer

Divisional Officer

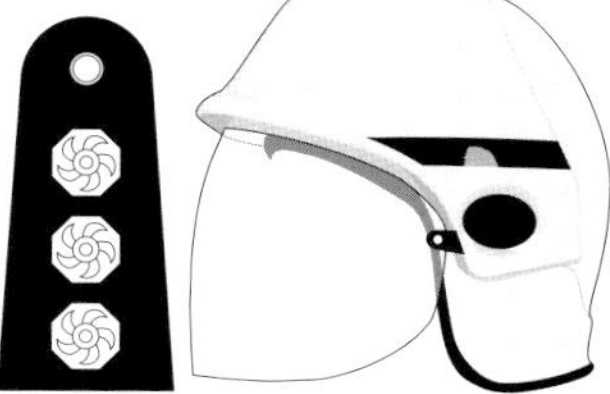
Assistant Divisional Officer

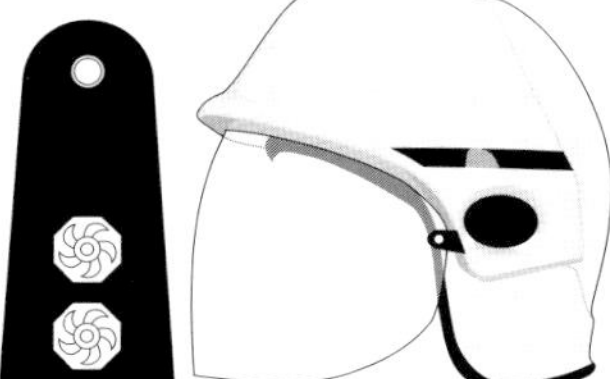
Station Officer

Sub Officer

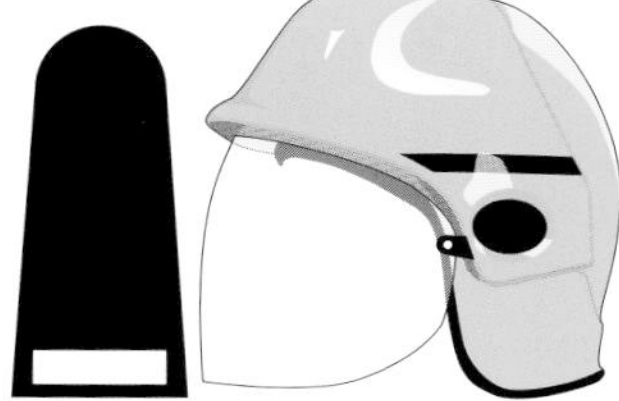
Leading Firefighter

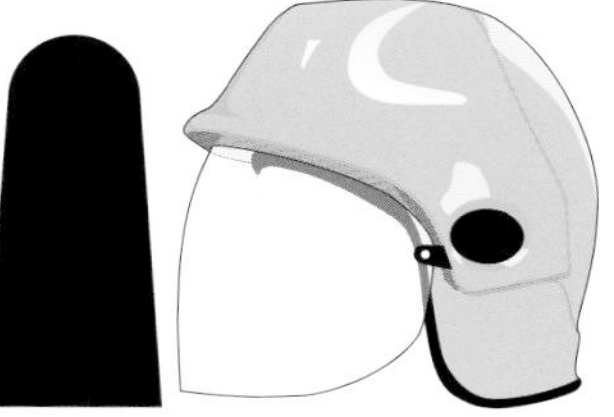
Firefighter

Ambulance Service Rank Insignia

Ambulance Service ranks are shown by shoulder strap slip-ons. They use military-style pips but senior officers have a device that features the Staff of Aesculapius, the international symbol for medicine.

The Ambulance Services in England and Wales have a single design of badge, differenced only by the name of the Service.

Chief Executive

Assistant Chief Officer

Sector Commander

Control Commander

Station Commander / Senior Duty Officer

Duty Officer

Team Leader

St John Ambulance Rank Insignia

Officer ranks are indicated by slides, normally black, but red for doctors, grey for nurses and green for paramedics. Senior officers have gorget patches.

Royal Appointment

Chief Commander

Deputy Chief Commander

Chief Officer

Deputy Chief Officer

Assistant Chief Officer

Commander

Commissioner / Deputy Commander

Officer Grade 1

Officer Grade 2

Officer Grade 3

Officer Grade 4

Officer Grade 5

Officer Grade 6

National Anthems

The Royal and National Anthem of the United Kingdom, and the Royal Anthem of all four of the constituent countries, is "God Save the Queen":

God save our gracious Queen,
Long live our noble Queen,
God save the Queen!
Send her victorious,
Happy and Glorious,
Long to reign over us;
God save the Queen!

Thy choicest gifts in store
On her be pleased to pour;
Long may she reign;
May she defend our laws,
And ever give us cause
To sing with heart and voice,
God save the Queen!

The National Anthem of England is "Land of Hope and Glory"
Music: Edward W. Elgar Lyrics: Arthur C. Benson

Land of Hope and Glory,
Mother of the free,
How shall we extol thee,
Who are born of thee,
Wider and still wider,
Shall thy bounds be set,
God who made thee mighty,
Make thee mightier yet,
God who made thee mighty,
Make thee mightier yet.

The National Anthem of Scotland is "Flower of Scotland"

Music & Lyrics: Roy Williamson

O Flower of Scotland,
When will we see your like again,
That fought and died for,
Your wee bit Hill and Glen,
And stood against him,
Proud Edward's Army,
And sent him homeward,
Tae think again.

The Hills are bare now,
And Autumn leaves lie thick
and still,
O'er land that is lost now,
Which those so dearly held,
That stood against him,
Proud Edward's Army,
And sent him homeward,
Tae think again.

Those days are past now,
And in the past they must
remain,
But we can still rise now,
And be the nation again,
That stood against him,
Proud Edward's Army,
And sent him homeward,
Tae think again.

O Flower of Scotland,
When will we see your like again,
That fought and died for,
Your wee bit Hill and Glen,
And stood against him,
Proud Edward's Army,
And sent him homeward,
Tae think again.

The National Anthem of Wales is "Hen Wlad fy Nhadau / Land of My Fathers"

Music: James James Welsh Lyrics: Evan James English Lyrics: Arthur L. Salmon

Cymraeg:

Mae hen wlad fy nhadau yn annwyl i mi,
Gwlad beirdd a chantorion, enwogion o fri;
Ei gwrol rhyfelwyr, gwladgarwyr tra mâd,
Tros ryddid collasant eu gwaed.

Gwlad, Gwlad, pleidiol wyf i'm gwlad,
Tra môr yn fur i'r bur hoff bau,
O bydded i'r heniaith barhau.

English:

Dear land of my fathers, whose glories were told
By bard and by minstrel who loved thee of old;
Dear country whose sires, that their sons might be free,
Have suffered and perished for thee!

Wales! Wales! Land of mist and wild,
Where'er I roam, though far from home,
The mother is calling her child.

The National Anthem of Northern Ireland is "Danny Boy":

Music: traditional Lyrics: Frederic Edward Weatherly

O Danny boy, the pipes, the pipes are calling
From glen to glen, and down the mountainside;
The summer's gone, and all the roses falling;
'Tis you, 'tis you must go, and I must bide.

But come ye back when summer's in the meadow,
Or when the valley's hushed and white with snow,
'Tis I'll be here in sunshine or in shadow,
O Danny boy, O Danny boy, I love you so!

But when ye come, and all the flowers are dying,
If I am dead, as dead I may well be,
Ye'll come and find the place where I am lying
And kneel and say an "Ave" there for me.

And I shall hear, though soft you tread above me,
And all my grave will warmer, sweeter be,
For you will bend and tell me that you love me,
And I shall sleep in peace until you come to me.

National Plants

The national plant of England is the rose, that of Scotland is the thistle, that of Northern Ireland is the shamrock and that of Wales is the leek or daffodil. They are normally shown on flags in a stylized heraldic form as shown here:

National Mottos

The national mottos of England and Scotland are those of their highest orders of chivalry. For England it is "*Honi Soit Qui Mal Y Pense*" - Evil To Him Who Thinks Evil - from the Order of the Garter. Scotland's is "*Nemo Me Impune Lacessit*" - No One Provokes Me With Impunity - from the Order of the Thistle. Wales uses "*Cymru Am Byth*" - Wales For Ever - and "*Pleidiol Wyf I'm Gwlad*" - True Am I To My Country. Northern Ireland has "*Quis Separabit*" - Who Will Separate Us - from the Order of St Patrick.

The Royal mottos are "*Dieu Et Mon Droit*" - God And My Right - for England, "*In Defens*" - In Defence - for Scotland and "*Y Ddraig Goch Ddyry Cychwyn*" - The Red Dragon Gives Impetus - for Wales.

Appendix A - Precedence of Flags

There are four main orders of flags in the United Kingdom, depending upon the occasion (note that normally only the most senior Royal flag is flown):

General Precedence

The Royal Standard
The Personal Flag of
- HRH The Duke of Edinburgh
- HRH The Prince of Wales
- HRH Prince William of Wales
- HRH Prince Harry of Wales
- HRH The Duke of York
- HRH The Earl of Wessex
- HRH The Princess Royal
- HRH The Duke of Gloucester
- HRH The Duke of Kent
- HRH Prince Michael of Kent
- HRH Princess Alexandra

The Other Members' Standard
The Union Flag
The White Ensign of the Royal Navy
The Ensign of the Royal Air Force
The Blue Ensigns
The Red Ensigns
National Flag of the host constituent nation, crown dependency or overseas territory
National Flags of other nations, including England, Scotland, Wales, crown dependencies and overseas territories (in English alphabetical order - see Appendix C)
The United Nations Flag
The Commonwealth Flag
The European Union Flag
The British Army Flag
Counties and Metropolitan Cities
Other Cities
Towns
Banners of Arms (both personal and corporate)
House Flags

Commonwealth Events (but not the Commonwealth Games) Order

Royal Standards (as above)
The Commonwealth Flag
The Union Flag
National Flag of the host constituent nation, crown dependency or overseas territory
National Flags of the Commonwealth in order of original accession to the Commonwealth

United Nations Events Order

The United Nations Flag
National Flags of the United Nations in order of their name as used at the UN. The exceptions to the normal alphabetical order are (with the sorting letter in red):
Côte d'Ivoire (was called Ivory Coast), Democratic People's Republic of Korea (North Korea), Republic of Korea (South Korea), Republic of Moldova (Moldova), The former Yugoslav Republic of Macedonia (Macedonia), Timor Leste (East Timor), United Republic of Tanzania (Tanzania)

European Union (and NATO) Events Order

The European Union (or NATO) Flag
National Flags in order of their name in their primary local language (countries only in the EU are in blue, countries only in NATO are in red, countries in both the EU and NATO are in black):
België / Belgique / Belgien (Belgium), *Canada*, *Ceska Republika* (The Czech Republic), *Danmark* (Denmark), *Deutschland* (Germany), *España* (Spain), *Eesti* (Estonia), *France*, *Hellás* (Greece), *Ireland*, *Ísland* (Iceland), *Italia* (Italy), *Kypros / Kibris* (Cyprus), *Latvija* (Latvia), *Lietuva* (Lithuania), *Luxembourg*, *Magyarország* (Hungary), *Malta*, *Nederland* (The Netherlands), *Norge* (Norway), *Österreich* (Austria), *Polska* (Poland), *Portugal*, *Slovenija* (Slovenia), *Slovensko* (Slovakia), *Suomi* (Finland), *Sverige* (Sweden), *Türkiye* (Turkey), *United Kingdom*, *United States*

United Nations

Appendix B - International Organizations

The United Kingdom is a member of numerous international organizations, including the United Nations (UN), the Commonwealth, the European Union (EU), the Council of Europe, the North Atlantic Treaty Organization (NATO), the Western European Union, the Secretariat of the Pacific Community (SPC), the International Olympic Committee (IOC) and the Commonwealth Games Federation. Through Montserrat it is a member of the Caribbean Community (CARICOM).

Commonwealth

North Atlantic Treaty Organization

Secretariat of the Pacific Community

European Union and Council of Europe

Western European Union

Caribbean Community

Appendix C - National Flags of Other Nations

To help with identification and international flag displays the flags of other nations are shown here in the normal English alphabetical order. The order uses the short name of the country rather than its formal name (ie. "Australia" rather than "Commonwealth of Australia") and ignores "The". Some of the names that might not be familiar are: Congo-Brazzaville - the old French colony of Congo; Congo-Kinshasa - the old Belgian Congo, now formally called the Democratic Republic of Congo; Côte d'Ivoire - the Ivory Coast; Myanmar - the modern name of Burma; and Serbia & Montenegro - formerly Yugoslavia.

Most of the flags shown here are the National Flag of the country concerned, but for some countries it is normal practice to use the State Flag (usually the National Flag with the addition of the country's arms) for all purposes outside the country, and for these the State Flag is shown.

Some of these countries are actually dependencies of other nations and these are marked with a dagger symbol (†). The flags marked with an asterix (*) represent 'nations' that are not internationally recognized. Care should be taken when using any of these flags as they may cause offence to representatives of other countries. For example, the Chinese are likely to be upset by a display of either the Tibet or Taiwan flags, and Moroccans may be annoyed at the Western Sahara flag.

The flags are correct as of February 2004 but it is always wise to check for flag changes. Up-to-date information on flag changes can be found on The Flag Institute's website (www.flaginstitute.org) or on The World Flag Database (www.flags.net). Most of the large flag makers also track changes to the world's flags and can advise purchasers.

Afghanistan

Åland Islands†

Albania

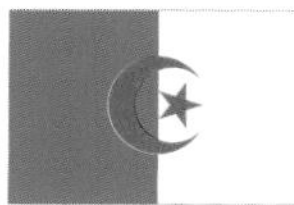
Algeria

American Samoa†

Andorra

Angola

Antigua & Barbuda

Argentina

Armenia

Aruba†

Australia

Austria

Azerbaijan

The Azores†

The Bahamas

Bahrain

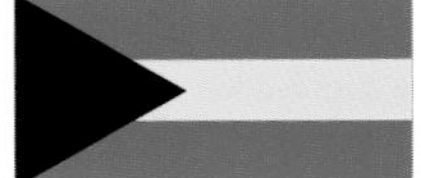
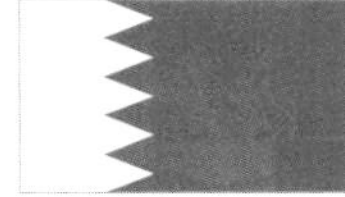
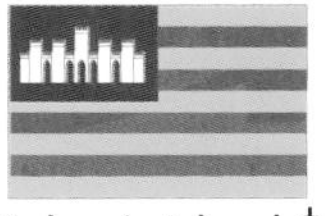
Balearic Islands†

Bangladesh

Barbados

Belarus

Belgium

Belize

Benin

Bhután

Bolivia

Bosnia & Herzegovina

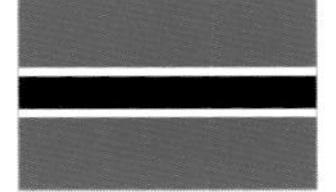
Botswana

Brazil

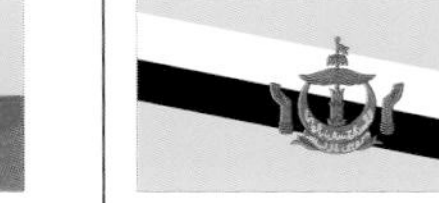

Brunei Darussalam

Bulgaria

Burkina Faso

Burundi

Cambodia

Cameroon

Canada

Canary Islands†

Cape Verde

Central African Republic

Chad

Chile

China

Christmas Island†

Colombia

Comoros

Congo-Brazzaville

Congo-Kinshasa

Cook Islands†

Costa Rica

Côte d'Ivoire

Croatia

Cuba

Cyprus

Czech Republic

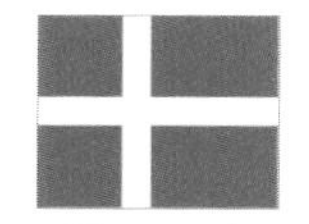
Denmark

Djibouti

Dominica

Dominican Republic

East Timor

Ecuador

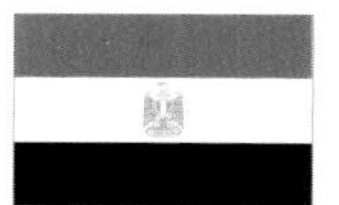
Egypt

El Salvador

Equatorial Guinea

Eritrea

Estonia

Ethiopia

Faroe Islands†

Fiji

Finland

France

French Polynesia†

Gabon

The Gambia

Georgia

Germany

Ghana

Greece

Greenland†

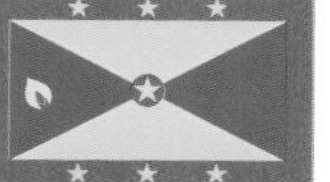
Grenada

Guam†

Guatemala

Guinea

Guinea-Bissau

Guyana

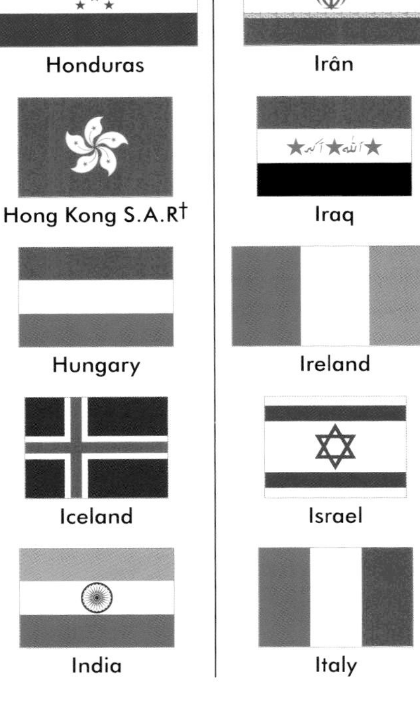

Haiti

Honduras

Hong Kong S.A.R†

Hungary

Iceland

India

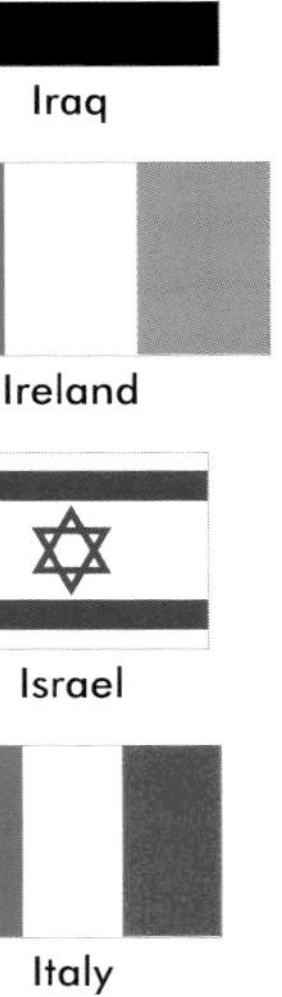

Indonesia

Irân

Iraq

Ireland

Israel

Italy

Jamaica

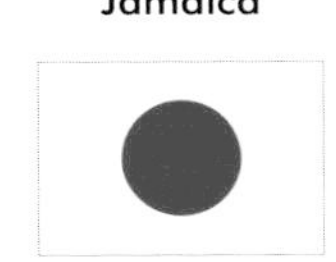

Japan

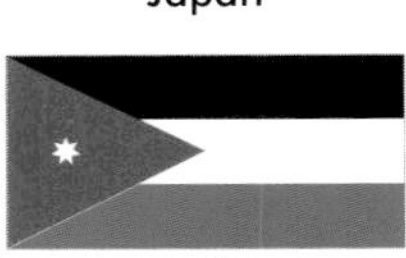

Jordan

Kazakhstan

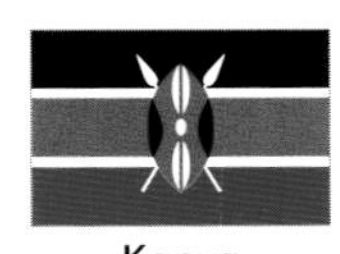

Kenya

Kiribati

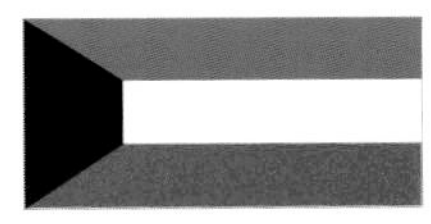

Kuwait

Kyrgyzstan

Laos

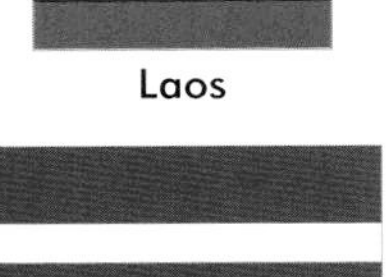

Latvia

Lebanon

Lesotho

Liberia

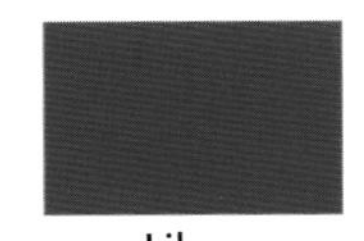

Libya

Liechtenstein

Lithuania

Luxembourg

Macau S.A.R†

Macedonia

Madagascar

Madeira†

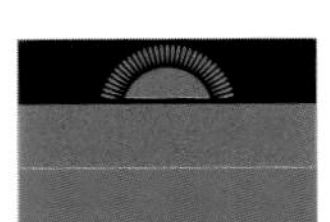
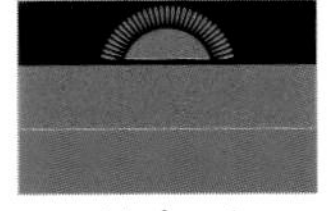

Malawi

Malaysia

Maldives

Mali

Malta

Marshall Islands

Mauritania

Mauritius

México

Micronesia

Moldova

Monaco

Mongolia

Morocco

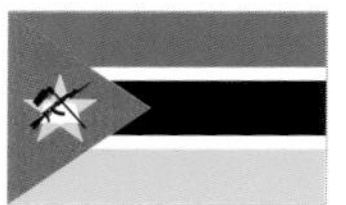
Mozambique

Myanmar

Namibia

Nauru

Nepal

Netherlands

Netherlands Antilles†

New Zealand

Nicaragua

Niger

Nigeria

Niue†

Norfolk Island†

North Korea

Northern Marianas†

Norway

Oman

Pakistan

Palau

Panamá

Papua New Guinea

Paraguay

Perú

Philippines

Poland

Portugal

Puerto Rico†

Qatar

România

Russian Federation

Rwanda

Saint Kitts & Nevis

Saint Lucia

Saint Vincent & the Grenadines

Samoa

San Marino

São Tomé & Príncipe

Saudi Arabia

Senegal

Serbia & Montenegro

Seychelles

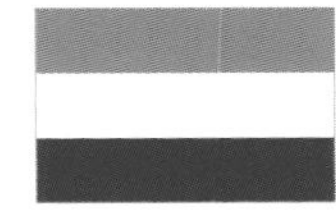
Sierra Leone

Singapore

Slovakia

Slovenia

Solomon Islands

Somalia

South Africa

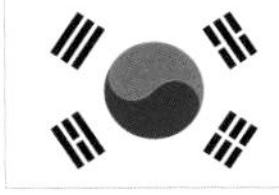
South Korea

Spain

Sri Lanka

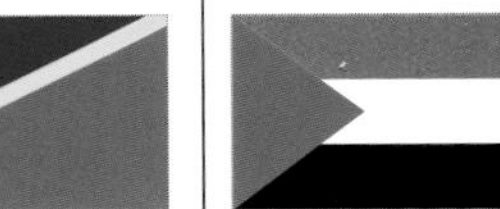
Sudan

Suriname

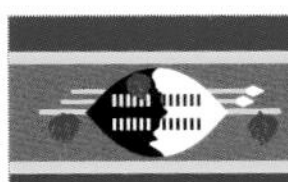
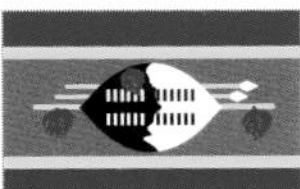
Swaziland

Sweden

Switzerland

Syria

Taiwan*

Tajikistan

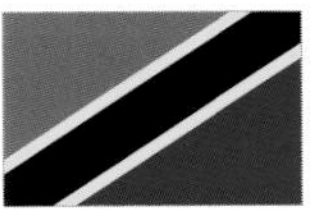
Tanzania

Thailand

Tibet*

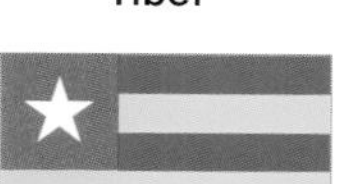
Togo

Tonga

Trinidad & Tobago

Tunisia

Turkey

Turkmenistan

Tuvalu

Uganda

Ukraine

United Arab Emirates

United States

Uruguay

Uzbekistan

Vanuatu

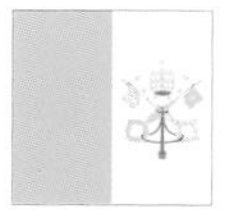
Vatican City

Venezuela

Viêt Nam

Virgin Islands†

Western Sahara*

Yemen

Zambia

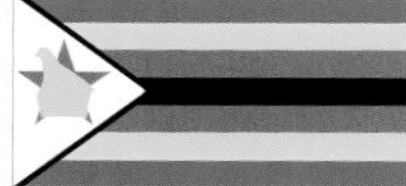
Zimbabwe

The Flag Institute

The Institute's Flag

The Flag of FIAV

The Flag Institute is the British vexillological organization, specializing in the study of flags past, present and future; a centre for excellence. It is a member of the *Fédération internationale des associations vexillogiques* (FIAV), the international flag organization.

The Institute publishes a quarterly journal, *Flagmaster*, that strives to include aspects of the world of flags, frequently presenting details and illustrations of new national and international flags.

The Flag Institute is always available to advise official organizations, private bodies and commercial companies on flag-related questions. The Institute's William Crampton Library is open to members and is based in Hull.

Membership of the Flag Institute is open to all those interested (private and corporate) in the world of flags. Meetings are held twice a year; the location of the meeting moves on each occasion to places of interest around the UK. To find out more please visit the Institute's website at www.flaginstitute.org

Robin Ashburner, President
David Lister, Vice-President
Cmdr Bruce Nicholls OBE RN, Vice-President
Sqn Leader Hugh Witherow MCMI, Vice-President
Cmdr Malcolm Farrow OBE FCMI RN, Chairman
Graham Bartram, General Secretary
Douglas Southern, Membership Secretary
Simon Bennett BA, Treasurer
Michael Faul BA FFI, Editor, *Flagmaster*
Lt Col Nick Weekes, Research Archivist
John Ford, Local Government & Byelaws
Rev John Hall BD, Ecclesiastical Flags
Brian Leigh Davis, Military Historian
Ray Allen, National Collections Liaison
Ian Sumner BA MCLIP, Librarian